W9-BGU-966

joshua weissman

an **unapologetic** cookbook

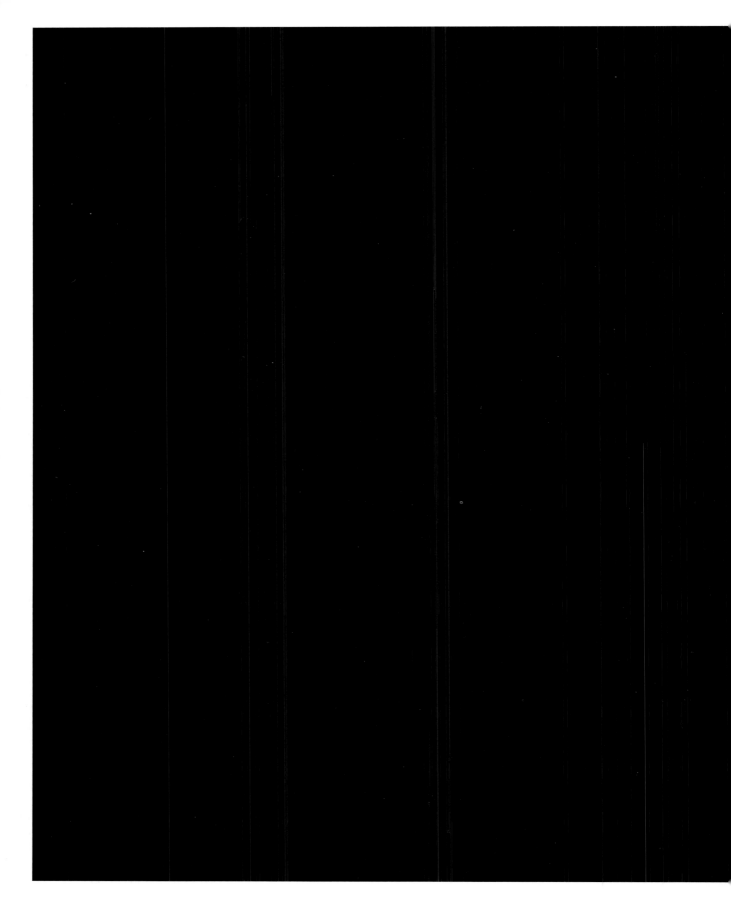

joshua
weissman

an **unapologetic** cookbook

Penguin
Random
House

Publisher Mike Sanders
Editor Alexandra Andrzejewski
Book Designer Rebecca Batchelor
Art Director for Photography Joshua Weissman
Photographer Ralph Smith
Producers for Supplementary Photography Vicram Chatterjee, Thomas J. Werner
Recipe Tester Ashley Brooks
Proofreader Lisa Starnes
Indexer Celia McCoy

First American Edition, 2021
Published in the United States by DK Publishing
6081 E. 82nd Street, Indianapolis, IN 46250

Library of Congress Catalog Number: 2021931009
ISBN: 978-1-6156-4998-3

DK books are available at special discounts when purchased
in bulk for sales promotions, premiums, fund-raising,
or educational use. For details, contact:
SpecialSales@dk.com

Printed and bound in Canada

For the curious

www.dk.com

for mom and dad

It would make zero sense for me to dedicate this to anyone but you. I feel immensely grateful to have two hardworking parents, who have done nothing but support my goals and dreams in every way possible.

contents

a little cooking foundation

foundations applied

an unapologetic introduction

Cooking is an art form. It's expressive. It's one of those things that separates us human beings from some ordinary animal...like that bird who keeps flying into your window over and over even though it's so inexplicably obvious that he isn't going to make it through on try #69. It's also a very, very touchy subject for a lot of people in a lot of different ways. But I think it's high time people come to terms with something: cooking isn't what it used to be. It's much, much better. As a matter of fact, the food and drink world is the most exciting and diversified it has ever been in the history of mankind... right now. We are living through it. And this is just the beginning. My point in this is one major thing: let's embrace and enjoy the evolution of food. This is something my Italian friends have a hard time doing...but we won't get into that. (Sorry guys, you know I love you. Just a light roast.)

What I want is for people to understand that right now, the number one most important thing you can have in your cooking arsenal is not some weird newfangled device whose only task is to dismantle a single avocado and literally nothing else. The most important thing is culinary intuition. If you understand how and why various cooking techniques and ingredients behave the way they do, then there is no boundary or barrier of entry for any idea you could ever have in food. But beyond that, I mean there are literally no rules at all. Yes, respect tradition, and yes, "get your reps in" and build a good baseline of understanding about proper cooking, cuisine, and most importantly technique... but it's time to stop putting the past on a pedestal, and just make something that's f—ing delicious.

—Chef Joshua Weissman

the unapologetic kitchen

Let me extrapolate a little here. I'm not saying there aren't facts in cooking and cuisine. I'm a big believer in proper and perfectly executed technique. I scrutinize my own on a regular basis. So for every culinary purist reading right now, please relax any tension in your body… maybe go get a massage and eat your caviar egg or something. I'm simply offering a new thought process that is built on a combination of legitimate facts (i.e., technique *X* produces result *Y)* and personal preference. That means you can't really fully understand this unless you begin to build your culinary intuition.

Why should you care? Well, there are a million reasons why you should care, but I'm also not going to spend a second trying to convince you. Instead, let me propose the following. Don't be that person on a date who, when the other person asks if you wanna cook dinner together, you have to admit to them you don't know what asparagus looks like. It's depressing, and yes, you should be just a little ashamed. I don't intend for that to sound like I'm bullying anyone, for the record. Of course you don't have to care; I'm only trying to offer you something that's the antithesis of the 2.3-second 1-ingredient meals that abound. One thing I have noticed is that cooking is arguably one of the most valuable experiences one can have. So why try to rush it in the first place? There are a lot of things in life you can't control, but the food you cook is one of the few things you can, and this gives you a real sense of power over a huge aspect of your life. But hey, take that as you will because, again, I don't care if you want to cook or not. My objective is just to be thought-provoking here.

Now, if you want to build intuition, then you've come to the right place. I wrote this book not to give you revolutionary recipes that nobody on the entire planet has ever seen, but instead to give you a very basic and open-ended path to experiencing food and recipes in one place. Some of these recipes are surprisingly easy, and some are surprisingly difficult. Ideally, you'll cook your way through the front half of this book by first making sauces, broths, cheeses, and more, most of which are foods familiar to you. You'll develop an understanding of how food is made. This builds that baseline and establishes the intuition you need in order to progress, but it also literally gives you the ingredients for the actual "full" recipes in the book. I believe they call these building blocks, but I've always felt like that's a really juvenile and overly simplified way to describe them. But sure, you can be a little baby, waving your tiny baby arms, tossing your nice-colored food blocks around.

food has to be built

No, not built like the robots that squirt sauce onto a burger, which will never form a single molecule of mold on it. I mean that just about anything you put in your mouth (please keep your dirty thoughts at bay here), from the ketchup you dip your fries in, to the fancy grocery store chocolate you eat, has to be built. Produce aside, at some point literally every food has to be pieced together in a balanced way to make it what it is. Most of the effort to do so, and the value it gives us, is lazily dismissed. You know how the saying goes: "You don't know what you've got till it's gone."

More importantly, you don't know how much better something can be when you make it. After all, you've been letting someone else make your pickles, breads, condiments, sauces, and just about every single food that makes up the flavor of your meals. For all you know, your favorite dill pickles may actually kind of suck compared to what they could be. (I hope this is triggering some form of FOMO at this point.) By the way, I don't want you to think you can't enjoy your favorite store-bought sauce. I'm only suggesting that making it yourself may bring you to a level that's perfectly made for you as an individual.

Now, take a step back. Each of these things you use on a daily basis had to be made with a list of ingredients in order to create its own...ingredient. But why can't we fully control and harness that power ourselves? Short answer: we can. I broke this book into a few very simple categories of food (*staples from scratch,* page 19, which includes broths, fats, cheeses, sauces, ferments, and more; and *breads & starches from scratch,* page 51, which includes a whole variety of loaves, biscuits, and other starchy foods), which fill a huge percentage of some of those things we often just buy without really understanding what goes into them.

From there, you can use your staples to build out the full recipes in the book or make up your own recipes. For example, maybe you make the burger buns, but you choose to use them for your own beautiful grilled fish sandwich with your choice of pickles and flavored mayo. There are unlimited combinations and possibilities here, people. The satisfying result is that you become a completely self-sustained cook with dozens of ingredients that can coincide with each other to make something greater than the sum of its parts.

staples from scratch

Remember when I said your favorite pickles might actually suck? Yeah, well, we can correct that in this first chapter (page 19). This part of the book is going to explain how to make some of the absolute foundations of many foods we eat and use every day, from a proper stock to pickles and jams. We even touch on cheese in this chapter (not just because I think everyone who cooks should know a little about cheese-making, but because it teaches a sense of appreciation for what it takes to make great cheese).

breads & starches from scratch

We allow other people to make bread for us, often without ever tasting the real, fresh thing (unless you frequent a legitimate local bakery). Not everyone wants to make their own bread, and I get that...but you are reading this section, so it seems to me that you might be a little curious about bread. Don't be shy; give it a try. If you fail miserably, be patient. I'm begging you. When you hit the mark on this, to me, it's a genuinely life-changing cooking scenario. It may take a few tries to get your first good loaf of bread. I know it can be intimidating, so keep reading to learn a little more.

The what's what of bread   There are hundreds of different kinds of breads, shaping techniques, fermentation techniques, enriching techniques, etc. The only things I want you to concern yourself with are two categories: sourdough bread and commercially yeasted bread. Before this gets overwhelming, let me start off with a reminder—the bread recipes I've included in this book are just to get you started; there are many different ways to go about making these doughs, so try to just focus on the way I'm giving them to you, and get fancy later.

- **Sourdough bread** in general is bread in which the rise and flavor composition are created solely through the process of fermentation. The caveat here is that sourdough bread takes time, and a lot of it, to make it good. The catalyst to this fermentation is your sourdough starter (page 52). The sourdough starter is literally just a symbiotic culture that contains a LOT of wild and naturally occurring yeast and healthy bacteria. There's a bunch of writing on the internet about what makes up a sourdough starter, but it's really just flour and water. In short, it provides lift to your bread.

- **Commercially yeasted bread** is any bread risen with instant or active dry yeast, or even those old-school solid blocks of fresh yeast. Commercially yeasted bread isn't (necessarily) fermented like sourdough bread, and the flavor isn't as deep. Instead, you have a very quickly risen dough that can handle a plethora of ingredients added to it. It's more versatile due to its neutral flavor. (I feel like the sourdough community pushes this type of yeast away too much. I simply don't want all of my breads to take 24 hours...I'm sorry. So you guys just need to leave my little *saccharomyces cerevisiae* ALONE!)

What I'd like to present is an opportunity to learn how to make both types of bread, taste the difference between them, and make them strategically based on what you want to eat.

Equipment   Most of these breads require pretty basic equipment, like loaf pans, baking sheets, etc. You can find these at grocery stores, kitchen equipment stores, and even restaurant supply stores (an underrated choice, in my opinion).

You'll probably want specialty equipment for the sourdough bread. I highly recommend acquiring two 10-inch (25-cm) round bannetons or two 9-inch (23-cm) batard bannetons, both of which you can buy online. I recommend getting ones that come with liners to avoid sticking. If you're a beginner, definitely start with the round banneton. If you end up making the big boy miche (page 57), you'll ideally want a 12-inch (30.5-cm) large wicker basket banneton. (I got mine at sfbi.com.) You'll want the one with the liner that can hold 3 to 3½ pounds (1.5–1.75kg) of dough. With all of that said, a bowl lined with a very large linen towel dusted with rice flour will do just fine if you want to limit shopping.

Ingredients   Bread is pretty simple. Proper sourdough literally only needs three ingredients: flour, water, and salt. Your flour choice greatly affects your outcome. All of the recipes in this book use unbleached flour. If your dough seems to be liquid-y, usually that means one of three things: you accidentally added too much liquid (happens more often than you think), the dough needs a lot more development, or your flour is weak. Test out different flours until you find one you like. I use my local H-E-B Organics and Central Milling for my all-purpose flour, bread flour, and sometimes whole wheat flour. For rye flour and most whole-grain flours, I usually use Bob's Red Mill or Central Milling.

The process   Let me keep this simple with a few definitions:

- **Rhubaud method:** I know this sounds like some sort of surgical trick a doctor uses when he doesn't know what else to do, but I assure you it's simple. This is kind of like kneading, but it's used for very wet and sticky doughs (typically for sourdough) to develop the gluten. This is performed in the bowl in which you're mixing the dough. Hold your hand in a cupped shape, reach under the dough, scoop half of it up, let it hang and stretch a little, and slap it back down into the bowl. You do this pretty quickly and aggressively, scooping it over and over again, until the dough reaches a stage of good tension, smoothness, and extensibility. It typically takes about 5 minutes, or sometimes twice that. This method exists basically to simulate the arm of a dough mixer, like the kind that costs thousands of dollars. Good thing using your hands is free.

- **Kneading:** The process of working a dough either on a counter or in a bowl by folding and pressing the dough onto itself repeatedly to develop the gluten and acquire tension and strength.

- **Rise or bulk ferment:** The initial rise of sourdough, before it is proofed, taking place over the course of several hours.

- **Proofing:** The second rise you apply to the dough. Once you shape the dough into its final shape, it needs to develop gas to hold its shape.

foundations applied

This is exactly what you think it is—the actual cookbook recipes (page 87). I include a mix of both traditional recipes (or my iteration thereof) and some completely brand-new recipes. Most of these recipes call for some of the staples you already made in the *a little cooking foundation* section (page 17).

The beauty is that if you made a bunch of the foundational recipes prior, you'll suddenly see how interconnected it all is. Obviously, many of those ingredients can also be acquired at the store; I'm not going to judge you. I'm merely giving you the OPTION to control every single aspect of the food you make. Should you choose this adventure, you'll experience food that is perfectly customized and optimized for you. But whatever...you can also just never experience that in your life and be completely fine.

15

a little cooking foundation

If you want to make anything in this book, you should probably try to fight the urge to avoid making the stuff in this first part. Plus, each recipe you complete will likely grow your ego, and that's a win in my book...literally.

staples from scratch

I could make this list go on forever...but I decided to spare you, or maybe spare myself the additional writing. Long story short, this isn't an exhaustive list by any means, but it does contain a bunch of things that you hopefully find familiar but have never thought to make yourself.

PREP TIME:
15 MINUTES + COOLING

COOK TIME:
10 MINUTES

YIELD:
1-QT (1-LITER) JAR

pickled anything

Not everything needs to be complicated. Pickles look complicated, but they're actually ridiculously easy. If you've ever wanted to make pickles at any point in your life, then that time has come.

Hardy fresh vegetables or fruits of choice (such as cucumbers, carrots, onions, white parts of green onions, hard peaches, radishes, etc.), cut to fit into the jar

Aromatics of choice (optional; such as fresh garlic, fresh herbs, black peppercorns, coriander seeds, bay leaves, juniper berries, whole spices, etc.)

All-purpose pickling liquid:
1½ cups (350ml) white distilled vinegar
1 cup (250ml) filtered water
1 tbsp (18g) kosher salt

note: To make **dill pickles,** in a 1-quart (1-liter) jar, add quartered kirby cucumbers, 4 sprigs dill, 5 cloves garlic, and 1 tablespoon (8g) black peppercorns.

CARROTS

1 Fill a 1-quart (1-liter) canning jar with the desired vegetables and any fresh herbs and garlic (for example, cucumbers and sprigs of sage), leaving a bit of headspace.

2 Make the all-purpose pickling liquid. In a medium pot, combine the vinegar, water, and salt. Add the desired aromatics, excluding fresh herbs and garlic. (For example, you could add Sichuan peppercorns, toasted coriander seeds, and mustard seeds.) Bring the mixture to a boil. As soon as the liquid comes to a boil and the salt is fully dissolved, turn off the heat.

3 Pour the hot pickling liquid with the aromatics directly over the vegetables until they are fully submerged. To keep the vegetables from floating, place a paper towel folded to fit in the top of the jar over the vegetables. Keep the jar uncovered, and let it cool to room temperature. Once the liquid has cooled completely, remove the paper towel and screw the lid onto the jar. Refrigerate. Your pickles are done and ready to be enjoyed at any time. These will last for several months in the refrigerator.

JALAPEÑOS

RED ONIONS

PREP TIME:
15 MINUTES

FERMENTATION TIME:
3–14 DAYS

YIELD:
1-QT (1-LITER) JAR

lacto-fermented vegetables

It sounds a little gross. I get it. Please understand that this is short for *lactobacillus*....
Okay, maybe I'm not helping myself here with the terminology. The point is that this
is a very simple ferment requiring nothing more than some salt, water, vegetables,
and a few days to develop tons of new flavors. Think of it kinda like old-school pickles,
but with way more depth of flavor. Plus, they're actually pretty good for you!

Hardy fresh vegetables (such as
  cucumbers, carrots, beets,
  cauliflower, cabbage, white
  asparagus, radishes, etc.; see
  notes), cut to fit into the jar

Filtered water
Fine sea salt (this dissolves better than
  kosher or coarse salt)

CAULIFLOWER

1 Place a wide-mouthed jar (at least
1 quart/1 liter, or whatever size best fits
your veggies) on a scale and zero out
the weight. Add the vegetables, leaving
a bit of headspace. Pour filtered water
into the jar just to cover the vegetables.
Record the total weight of the water
and vegetables in grams.

2 Based on the vegetables you're
using, determine the percentage of
salt you need in your brine. (Use
2 percent salt for most vegetables,
but increase this to 3 percent for
vegetables with higher water content
that are prone to mold, such as
cucumbers and peppers.) Multiply
the weight recorded in step 1 by the
brine percentage (either 0.02 or 0.03)
to get the amount of salt you need in
grams. (For example, if the vegetables
plus water weigh 1,500 grams,
multiply that by 2 percent, which
comes out to 30 grams. You would
need 30 grams salt in this scenario.)

**CUCUMBERS
WITH DILL**

3 Prepare the brine. Pour the water from the jar into a large bowl. Add salt to the water, and stir until the salt is fully dissolved.

4 Once dissolved, pour the brine over the vegetables in the jar. Weigh down the vegetables so they are fully submerged, using either fermentation weights, nonmetallic pinch bowls, or a small resealable bag partially filled with water. If your vegetables aren't floating too much, you can simply use a little bit of plastic wrap that adheres to the surface of the liquid.

5 Lightly screw on the lid, but not too tight. An airtight jar could trap the gases and cause the jar to explode.

6 Let the vegetables rest at room temperature until they have reached the desired taste, typically between 3 days and 2 weeks. You'll notice the brine start to turn cloudy—this is a good thing. To store, leave the vegetables in the brine with the lid screwed on tightly and refrigerate for a *very* long time.

notes: Some vegetables ferment more efficiently than others. This is due to a lot of factors, so just play around with veggie types and fermentation times until you find some combinations that turn out well. I usually prefer to lacto-ferment a single vegetable type in the jar so its flavor is highlighted in its true state.

If you get a fuzzy, patchy mold, just throw out the batch and start again. However, a weblike white substance called kahm yeast might also develop on the surface. This is not mold, so you can still eat your fermented veggies.

GREEN BEANS

RED CHILIES

PREP TIME:
30 MINUTES

COOK TIME:
30 MINUTES

YIELD:
1 CUP

simple jams

I understand why most people opt not to make their own jam. It has to be hard, right? Well, actually no, that's wrong...sorry, bud.

2 lb (1kg) fresh fruit
  (see note)
2½ cups (500g) granulated
  sugar
⅓ cup (75ml) fresh lemon
  juice

1 Cut the fruit into bite-sized pieces and place in a medium saucepan. Add the sugar, and stir to coat completely. Let sit at room temperature for 20 minutes. (This is called *maceration* and helps extract juices and activate the natural pectin in your fruit.)

2 Once macerated, stir in the lemon juice. Place over medium-high heat, and bring to a boil. Continue boiling, stirring regularly, for 10 to 15 minutes, or until reduced.

**APPLE
JAM**

note: You can use most hardy fruits, but ultra high–sugar fruits such as banana or pineapple require significantly less added sugar. I recommend sticking to berries, stone fruits, or apples. Obviously, if you're using something with a pit in it, remove the pit before cutting the fruit (if that wasn't already evident…).

3 Once the mixture turns lightly syrupy, test it by drizzling some on a clean plate. Let it cool, and mix it around on your fingers. If it makes a light, sticky string when you pull your fingers apart, it's done. If not, keep cooking longer, up to 15 more minutes.

4 Prepare an ice bath in a large bowl. Transfer the jam to a medium bowl, and set the bowl inside the ice bath. Stir the mixture until it's completely cold. Store tightly covered in jars in the refrigerator for up to 1 month.

PLUM JAM

STRAWBERRY JAM

PREP TIME:
10 MINUTES + COOLING

COOK TIME:
10 MINUTES

YIELD:
1½ CUPS

nut butters

Aside from laughing at the term *nut butter,* this is yet another staple that has huge benefits to making it yourself at home. The biggest benefit by far is CONTROL. You can control how chunky or smooth it is. You can add more or less salt. Plus, you can tell all your friends you make nut butter, and none of them will ever come over again.

2½ cups (280g) raw nuts
¾ tsp (5g) kosher salt
  (optional; use more or
  less to taste)

**HAZELNUT
BUTTER**

**CASHEW
BUTTER**

1   Preheat the oven to 350°F (180°C). Line a baking sheet with parchment paper.

2   Spread the nuts evenly across the baking sheet. Roast for about 10 minutes, shaking the pan occasionally, until the nuts are fragrant and lightly toasted. Let the roasted nuts cool to room temperature.

3   Place the nuts in a food processor. Process on high speed for up to 15 minutes, scraping down the sides as necessary, until the nuts are blended into a butter and as smooth as you like it.

4   Once the nut butter is the consistency you like, blend in the salt (if using). If you'd like a chunky nut butter, pulse in a handful or two of whole nuts until it's your desired consistency.

5   Pour your nut butter (haha) into an airtight container, and store in the refrigerator for up to 1 month.

ALMOND BUTTER

27

PREP TIME:
5 MINUTES

COOK TIME:
**4 HOURS
40 MINUTES**

YIELD:
**ABOUT 2 QT
(2 LITERS)**

basic stock out of anything

Let's face it...buying stock or broth at the store 9/10 times is kind of depressing. You're basically just buying water. Oh yeah, sure, sure, "batch slow-cooked for 12 hours," and yet it has the smell of cow hoof and the flavor of stale water. Making it yourself is usually going to be astronomically better, and best of all, you can just make a bunch and freeze it. You can mix up the vegetables and aromatics with whatever is on hand.

3–4 lb (1.5–2kg) chicken, beef, or pork bones (see notes)
Neutral-tasting oil, to coat
1 medium yellow onion, roughly chopped
1 large rib celery, roughly chopped
1 large carrot, roughly chopped
½ bunch of thyme or sage (optional)
Filtered water, to cover (4–5 qt/4–4.75 liters)

1 Preheat the oven to 425°F (220°C) on convection or 450°F (230°C) on conventional heating. Line a baking sheet with foil. Evenly arrange the bones on the sheet. Lightly drizzle the bones with oil, and rub it in to coat completely. Roast the bones for 30 to 40 minutes, or until deeply browned.

2 Place the roasted bones in a 5- to 6-quart (4.75–5.5-liter) stockpot. (The pot should be no more than three-quarters full.) Add the onion, celery, carrot, and thyme (if using). Pour filtered water into the pot just until it covers the bones and vegetables completely.

3 Heat over medium-high heat, uncovered. As soon as it reaches a boil, immediately reduce the heat to low and gently simmer for 3 to 4 hours, partially covered, stirring occasionally. While the stock is simmering, skim off any scum that rises to the top. Do not let it return to a boil.

4 After 3 to 4 hours, remove the bulk of the bones with tongs, and strain the stock through a mesh strainer into a heatproof container. Discard the solids. Cool the broth completely to room temperature. Portion the stock into freezer-proof airtight containers, and freeze until needed.

notes: It's great to pick bones that still have a little bit of meat attached to them. That will contribute massively to the final flavor when you brown it in the oven.

Never salt your stock. Otherwise, anytime you use it, you risk overseasoning whatever it is you're making. Take the guesswork out of it.

STAPLES FROM SCRATCH

PHO
BROTH

BEEF STOCK

PORK STOCK

CHICKEN
STOCK

DASHI

PREP TIME:
30 MINUTES

COOK TIME:
ABOUT 5 HOURS

YIELD:
3–4 QT (3–4 LITERS)

pho broth

This is exactly what you think it is. It's the baseline of a beautiful bowl of nearly proper pho. Now, I want to make an important note here: this recipe exists solely for the purpose of making pho. But does that mean you can't get creative and make some steamed dumplings and then pop them in a shallow bowl of this hot broth? The answer is you can do whatever the hell you want with this broth. Be free, my child; be free.

5–6 lb (2.25–2.75kg) beef bones (knuckle and marrow)

Cooking spray, to coat

1 large whole knob of ginger

2 large yellow onions

Neutral-tasting oil, to coat

1–1½ lb (450–680g) chuck roast

Cold filtered water, to cover (5½ qt/5.25 liters)

5 cloves, toasted

5–6 whole star anise, toasted

3 black cardamom pods (optional)

⅓ cup (35g) coriander seeds, toasted

1 cinnamon stick, toasted

¼ cup (60ml) fish sauce, plus more to taste

1½ tbsp (20g) light brown sugar, plus more to taste

Stems from 1 bunch of cilantro (reserve the leaves for topping **beef pho, page 222**)

1 Preheat the oven to 425°F (220°C). Arrange the bones in an even layer on a foil-lined baking sheet. Spray lightly with cooking spray. Cook for 30 to 40 minutes, or until deep brown.

2 Once the bones are roasted, preheat the broiler. Cut the knob of ginger lengthwise into 2 thin pieces, leaving the skin on. Quarter the onions, leaving the skins on. Evenly arrange the ginger and onion on a foiled-lined baking sheet, skin-sides down. Lightly coat in oil. Broil for 10 to 12 minutes, turning occasionally, or until charred on the cut sides.

3 Lightly coat the bottom of a large sauté pan with oil. Heat over high heat until very hot. Sear each side of the chuck roast 2 to 3 minutes per side, or until browned. Set aside.

4 In a large stockpot, add the roasted bones and cover with the cold filtered water. Let them sit in the cold water for 5 minutes. (This step is crucial—it releases the albumin to help clarify the stock.) After 5 minutes, place the pot on the stove and slowly bring it up to a light simmer. (Don't let it boil.) Using a fine-mesh skimmer, intermittently skim off any foam and scum.

5 Once it comes to a light simmer, add the pieces of onions and ginger, seared chuck roast, cloves, star anise, black cardamom pods (if using), coriander seeds, cinnamon stick, fish sauce, and brown sugar. Stir to combine. Let simmer, uncovered, for 2 hours.

6 After 2 hours, carefully remove the chuck roast and refrigerate until needed or up to 4 days. Continue to simmer the broth for 2 hours more, uncovered. Intermittently skim off any fat that's risen to the top.

7 After simmering, remove all the bones to a large bowl. Into a very large bowl, carefully strain the broth through a mesh strainer. Season to taste with fish sauce and brown sugar. Save any extra meat and bone marrow before discarding the solids; refrigerate these items until needed, or up to 4 days.

8 While the broth is still hot, wrap the cilantro stems in cheesecloth and close with kitchen twine. Add the stems to the broth and let steep for 15 minutes. Remove and discard the stems. Use immediately for beef pho (page 222) or refrigerate in an airtight container for up to 5 days.

PREP TIME:
15 MINUTES

COOK TIME:
20 MINUTES

YIELD:
1 QT (1 LITER)

dashi

If chicken stock is in your repertoire of recipes and dashi isn't, then we are going to have a problem. Well, I mean you're going to have a problem. Dashi is arguably one of the most versatile ingredients you could possibly imagine in the world of Japanese food. It's great for ramen (page 226) or homemade miso soup.

1 qt (1 liter) filtered water
2 (2-inch/5-cm) pieces kombu
¾ cup (10g) bonito flakes

1 To a small saucepan, add the filtered water and kombu. Cook over medium-low heat until steaming, being careful not to bring it to a simmer or a boil. (A simmer will cause the kombu to make the liquid slimy.) Once it reaches a steamy heat, maintain that temperature for 10 minutes.

2 Once steeped, turn off the heat and add the bonito flakes. Cover and steep for 10 minutes more.

3 Strain the broth through a fine-mesh sieve, and discard the solids. Let the liquid cool to room temperature. Use immediately, store in an airtight container in the refrigerator for up to 1 week, or freeze indefinitely.

PREP TIME:
5 MINUTES

COOK TIME:
30 MINUTES TO 1 HOUR

YIELD:
VARIES

extracted animal fat

Pulling pure liquid fat from your fatty animal meat is a really straightforward process; don't overcomplicate it. This method will work with any solid animal fat you can think of. Use the extracted fats anytime you need cooking fat, like for frying or sautéing.

2–3 lb (1–1.5kg) animal fat from raw meat, such as fatty pork, beef, chicken, duck, etc.

1 Trim off any excess meat attached to the fat. Chop the solid raw fat into very small pieces. (For an even faster process, you can run the fat through a meat grinder attachment on a stand mixer.)

2 To a deep cast-iron sauté pan or small pot, add the finely chopped or ground fat. Heat over medium-low heat, and cook, stirring occasionally, for 30 minutes to 1 hour. You'll notice liquid fat begin to extract from the whole pieces of fat. Once the whole pieces of fat have reduced to crispy little pebbles, you've extracted all the fat you can.

3 Strain the animal fat through a fine-mesh sieve, and discard the solids. Store in an airtight container at room temperature or in the refrigerator indefinitely.

LARD
(PORK
FAT)

DUCK
FAT

CHICKEN
FAT

PREP TIME:
10 MINUTES

YIELD:
ABOUT 2 CUPS

unsalted butter

Starting today, you're not allowed to cook unless you know how butter is made. Okay, maybe that's a bit extreme, but my point is that this is an essential learning process. You should know what makes arguably one of the greatest foods on the planet.

3½ cups (875ml) heavy whipping cream (highest quality possible, ideally from a local source)

3 tbsp (45ml) ice-cold filtered water

1 In a food processor, process the heavy whipping cream on high speed for 3 to 6 minutes, or until very chunky and separated. As soon as the solids come together, it's done.

2 Strain the processed cream through a fine-mesh sieve and discard the whey (or save for another use). Add the butter solids back to the food processor. Add the ice water, and process on high speed once more for another 1 or 2 minutes to pull out any excess liquid.

3 Strain again. Gently gather up the butter solids and squeeze together to drain out any excess liquid. (You can also press it in a bowl with the back of a spoon to help express as much liquid as possible.)

4 The butter is done. You can mix in salt or flavorings (see note or *compound butters, page 35*), if you want. Otherwise, shape as desired. Refrigerate in an airtight container for up to 1 week, or freeze indefinitely.

note: To make **salted butter,** stir in 2 teaspoons (12g) salt of choice in step 4.

SPICY
KIMCHI
BUTTER

GARLIC-
HERB
BUTTER

CHAI
BUTTER

MSG
BUTTER

PREP TIME:
5 MINUTES + MAKING BUTTER (IF DESIRED)

YIELD:
1 CUP

compound butters

A *compound butter* is a nice culinary term to describe a flavored butter. It's not only underrated, but it's also underutilized. If you keep a couple flavored butters in your fridge, you can impart those flavors by adding the butter into a nice sauce, mixing it into your mashed potatoes, or even slathering it on toast to make some garlic bread. You see where I'm going here?

MSG butter:
1 cup (224g) **unsalted butter (page 33),** room temperature
2 tsp (8g) MSG
2 tsp (12g) fine sea salt
2 cloves garlic, grated

Garlic-herb butter:
1 cup (224g) **unsalted butter (page 33),** room temperature
4 cloves garlic, grated
2 tsp (12g) fine sea salt
2 tsp (6g) freshly cracked black pepper
½ cup (30g) finely chopped flat-leaf parsley
1 tbsp (5g) finely chopped thyme leaves
½ cup (124g) freshly, finely grated Parmigiano-Reggiano cheese

Spicy kimchi butter:
1 cup (224g) **unsalted butter (page 33),** room temperature
½ cup (120g) whole kimchi (drained), puréed in a food processor or blender
1 green onion, very finely chopped (almost a paste)
1 tbsp (15g) gochujang
1 tsp (6g) fine sea salt

Chai butter (best for sweet applications):
1 cup (224g) **unsalted butter (page 33),** room temperature
2 tsp (5g) ground cinnamon
1 tsp (2g) ground ginger
½ tsp (1g) ground nutmeg
1 tsp (2g) coriander seeds, toasted and ground
1 tsp (2g) cardamom, toasted and ground
1 tsp (6g) fine sea salt

1 In a medium bowl, add all of the ingredients for your desired butter flavor. Fold together until thoroughly incorporated and you have a smooth butter with no lumps.

2 Lay out a 1-foot- (30.5-cm-) long sheet of plastic wrap. Add the butter mixture in a mound in the center, and spread it into a 6-inch (15.25-cm) log. Carefully roll up the plastic wrap to form a cylinder of butter encased in the plastic.

3 Clamping the 2 ends of the plastic wrap with your fingers, slowly roll the log back and forth in a straight line along the counter until it develops enough tension to make an evenly shaped log.

4 Enjoy on or in whatever you'd like! Store wrapped in the refrigerator for up to 1 week.

PREP TIME:
30 MINUTES + 15–20 MINUTES TO REST

COOK TIME:
20 MINUTES

YIELD:
2–3 (5–6 OZ/140–170G) BALLS

mozzarella

Mozzarella is, in my opinion, one of the greatest cheeses to ever live. It goes with so many different things. It makes pizza what it truly deserves to be, it comforts you when you're sad, and it's the true hero of our world. Now imagine if you were able to harness that power.

1½ tsp (8g) citric acid (see notes)

1¼ cups (310ml) filtered water, divided

½ tsp (3g) liquid rennet (see notes)

1 gal (3.7 liters) cold whole milk (raw or pasteurized but not ultra-pasteurized; see notes)

1 tbsp (18g) kosher salt

1 In a small bowl, stir together the citric acid and 1 cup (250ml) filtered water until the citric acid is dissolved. In another small bowl, stir together the liquid rennet and the remaining ¼ cup (60ml) water.

2 In a large lidded pot, vigorously whisk together the cold whole milk with the citric acid mixture until well combined. Heat the milk over medium-low heat, uncovered, occasionally stirring very gently with a large spoon, until it reaches 90°F (32°C).

3 Immediately remove from the heat. Stirring constantly but gently, pour in the liquid rennet mixture. Once the rennet hits the milk, stir constantly and gently for another 25 seconds to thoroughly incorporate and then stop stirring. (Stirring too long will break up the curd.)

4 Place the lid on the pot, and let it sit at room temperature for 5 minutes. After 5 minutes, if you gently tilt the pot, you should see the solid curd distinctly floating on top. If not, let it sit for another 5 minutes, or until the curd is solidly on top.

5 Using a long knife, gently cut the curd in a crosshatch pattern (roughly 6 slits in the curd in each direction), making sure to go all the way to the bottom of the pot. (The curd moves very easily in the whey, so work slowly. You may need to use another utensil, such as a spatula, to help keep the curd steady.)

6 Place the pot back over medium-low heat. Heat, occasionally stirring very gently so you don't break the curds, until it reaches 105°F (40°C). Remove from the heat and let rest for 5 minutes, uncovered.

7 After 5 minutes, using a slotted ladle or small fine-mesh strainer, remove the curds to a strainer to drain for about 15 seconds. Using your hands, gently squeeze out some of the excess whey from the curd. (You don't have to get all the whey out.) Place the curd in a medium bowl.

Step 5

Step 9

Step 10

8 Season the whey left in the large pot with the salt. Heat the whey mixture to 180°F (82°C). Pour the heated whey over the curds until the curds are covered. Let sit for 15 to 20 seconds, or until the cheese is soft enough to form.

9 Once the cheese is softened, pick it up and pull it outward to stretch. (It is very hot, so use clean kitchen gloves to more easily tolerate the heat.) Fold the cheese over itself in half, and repeat this folding and stretching method until you have one smooth, even mass. It should take 4 to 6 folds. If at any point it gets too cold to form, simply heat it up again.

10 There are two ways to shape the mozzarella. One method is to form your thumb and fingers in a "C" shape and press a segment through your fingers to form a ball. Once you reach the desired size, pinch it off. Place into a container with room temperature whey completely covering the ball, and repeat with the rest of the mozzarella.

11 Alternatively, you can shape it by taking the desired amount and repeatedly folding the bottom over itself until a taut ball is formed. Then pinch the bottom shut. Place into a container with room temperature whey covering the ball, and repeat with the rest of the mozzarella.

12 Let the mozzarella balls rest in the room temperature whey for 15 to 20 minutes before serving. It's best served at room temperature within a few hours of making it. Wrap leftovers individually in plastic wrap, and refrigerate for up to 4 days.

notes: I know that the type of milk I'm asking for is a bit of a stretch (no pun intended), but you really need a low-temp pasteurized, if not *raw*, milk; otherwise, this just won't work. Lots of local farms sell this, and you can even find low-temp pasteurized milks at specialty stores like Whole Foods.

The same thing goes for citric acid and rennet. You can find those at health food markets and various other specialty grocery stores.

ricotta

Ricotta is literally the easiest cheese you can make. That's all I have to say.

½ gal (1.9 liters) whole milk (raw or pasteurized but not ultra-pasteurized; see notes on page 37)
¾ cup (175ml) heavy whipping cream
2½ tsp (15g) kosher salt
2½–4½ tbsp (40–70ml) white distilled vinegar

1 In a large pot, thoroughly whisk together the milk, cream, and salt. Heat the milk mixture over medium heat until it reaches 200°F (93°C), stirring occasionally so the milk doesn't burn on the bottom of the pot.

2 Once the mixture has reached the temperature, while constantly whisking, slowly stream in 2½ tablespoons (40ml) vinegar. You should start to see the curd and whey separating. Add up to 2 tablespoons (30ml) more vinegar if needed to curdle. Then immediately remove from the heat and let sit for 15 to 20 minutes. While it's cooling, place a metal sieve over a bowl, and line the sieve with cheesecloth.

3 Strain the mixture through the cheesecloth, and let sit for 15 minutes to 1 hour. The longer it sits, the firmer your ricotta will become. (I like 15 to 25 minutes.)

4 Once strained to your liking, carefully remove the cheesecloth from the sieve and turn the ricotta into a medium bowl. Adjust the seasoning as desired, and gently mix together. Store in an airtight container in the refrigerator for up to 1 week.

chèvre

If you can't find the right goat milk, keep this recipe on the back burner until you do!

1 qt (1 liter) goat milk (as unprocessed as possible, but avoid unpasteurized)
¼ cup (60ml) fresh lemon juice
3 tbsp (45ml) white distilled vinegar
1 tsp (6g) fine sea salt

1 Line a fine-mesh sieve with two layers of cheesecloth, and set over a bowl. In a heavy-bottomed saucepan, heat the goat milk over medium heat, stirring occasionally, until it reaches 180°F (82°C). Remove from the heat, add the lemon juice, and stir just a couple of times. Add the vinegar, and stir briefly just to combine. Let sit undisturbed for 30 minutes.

2 Gently stir in the salt. Slowly ladle the mixture into the cheesecloth. Gather the ends of the cheesecloth, bring together so it creates a hanging ball, tie those ends together, and tie it to a faucet or a cabinet handle. Let drip over the sink or into a bowl for 45 minutes to 1 hour.

3 Place the drained cheese on a sheet of plastic wrap. Loosely form into a log. Wrap the plastic wrap around it, and tighten each end to form the cheese into a tight log. Refrigerate for a couple of hours or overnight until set. Store tightly wrapped in the refrigerator for up to 1 week.

RICOTTA

CHÈVRE

MOZZARELLA

ALL-
PURPOSE
BARBECUE
SAUCE

MAYONNAISE

PESTO
SAUCE

HOT SAUCE

KETCHUP

PREP TIME:
10 MINUTES

FERMENTATION TIME:
2–4 DAYS

YIELD:
2 CUPS

hot sauce

I think hot sauce is properly rated. Not overrated, and not quite underrated. It's loved by many, and it's applicable to nearly anything. This hot sauce was made to be exactly what the title says it is...basic enough that it's pretty hot, but not mind-numbingly hot (depending on your personal tolerance). It's familiar, but with even more flavor than you could have imagined. This sauce really takes on the flavor of the chilies you choose to use. Experiment and find something you like.

1½ lb (680kg) red Fresno chilies (or whichever chilies you prefer: jalapeño, serrano, habanero, etc.), stemmed

5 cloves garlic

1½ tbsp (27g) kosher salt

5 tbsp (67g) light brown sugar

½ cup (125ml) white distilled vinegar, plus more if needed

3 tbsp (45ml) ume plum vinegar

⅛ tsp (0.5g) xanthan gum

1 Add the chilies and garlic to a food processor. Pulse until you get a roughly chopped consistency and then add the salt and brown sugar. Process on high speed until you get a coarse paste.

2 Transfer the paste to a canning jar (see note). Place the lid on top, but do not tighten or screw it on so air can escape, and let it ferment at room temperature for 2 to 4 days. Once the paste smells fragrant with a bit of a fermented nose, it's done.

3 Place the chili paste in a blender, along with the distilled vinegar and ume plum vinegar. Blend on high speed until as smooth as possible, adding more distilled vinegar if needed to thin. While the motor is running, blend in the xanthan gum.

4 Strain the mixture through a fine-mesh strainer into a jar or bottle, and discard the solids. It's ready to use in whatever you'd like. Store loosely covered in the refrigerator for a very long time.

> **note:** Use a cleaned and sanitized jar when making this. Because we are fermenting, it's best to keep a good eye on it and not let any foreign bacteria in. On the off chance of mold forming only on the surface, you can scrape it off. However, if more than that occurs, then restart.

ketchup

Yet another "Oh Josh, why even waste my time making my own ketchup?" First off, when did your time become more important than ketchup? Second off, the reason we make our own is so that we can control every variable of flavor to ultimately create our ideal ketchup that can be leveraged in so many amazing ways. So we have to do it.

1 (6 oz/170g) can tomato paste
½ cup (125ml) light corn syrup (see note)
¼ cup (60ml) white distilled vinegar
¼ cup (60ml) sherry vinegar
¼ cup (60ml) filtered water
2 tsp (7g) garlic powder
1 tsp (2g) onion powder
1 tbsp (18g) kosher salt

1 In a medium saucepan, stir together all of the ingredients. Place over medium-high heat. As soon as it begins to bubble, immediately reduce the heat to medium-low. Let the mixture simmer and reduce, stirring occasionally, for 4 to 5 minutes, or until reduced and glossy.

2 Transfer to a separate container. Cool completely, covered with a lid or plastic wrap so it doesn't form a skin. It's ketchup...you know how to use it. (And if you don't, there are lots of recipes in the book.) Store in an airtight container in the refrigerator for up to 1 month.

note: I know a lot of you might be thinking, "Oh my gosh, Josh is using corn syrup?????" Relax. You can absolutely use granulated sugar, but the best way to get the classic ketchup flavor and glossy texture is with a light corn syrup. Not high fructose; just light. No healthy and perfect-tasting ketchup really truly exists, so just don't eat half a cup of this stuff every day, and you'll be just fine.

pesto sauce

This might be considered sacrilege by the purists and traditionalists out there. This method of making pesto sauce goes directly against the Genovese Italian grandmother way of doing things. By blending the sauce and emulsifying it with olive oil (instead of making it traditionally by hand), you end up with a rich, thick, almost creamy sauce that coats any pasta absolutely beautifully but retains the rich, full-body flavor a pesto should have.

⅓ cup (45g) raw pine nuts
2 cups (40g) firmly packed basil
5 cloves garlic, peeled
1 cup (248g) freshly grated Parmigiano-Reggiano cheese
Kosher salt and freshly cracked black pepper, to taste
Splash of filtered water
½ cup (125ml) extra-virgin olive oil

1 To a small cold saucepan, add the pine nuts. Heat over medium heat, stirring often, for 2 to 3 minutes, or until the pine nuts are lightly toasted. Cool completely.

2 To a blender, add the basil, whole garlic cloves, Parmigiano-Reggiano, salt and pepper to taste, and the toasted pine nuts.

3 Begin blending on high speed, and add a small splash of water to help loosen the mixture. Once it is smooth, while the blender is running on high speed, begin streaming in the oil until the desired consistency is reached.

4 Immediately transfer to a separate container, and season to taste with salt and pepper. If using the pesto sauce at a later date, immediately cool it in an ice bath. Store in an airtight container (with plastic wrap pressed against the surface) in the refrigerator for up to 1 week.

PREP TIME:
**5 MINUTES + MAKING
KETCHUP (IF DESIRED)**

COOK TIME:
15–20 MINUTES

YIELD:
2 CUPS

all-purpose barbecue sauce

Whether you need it to top a nice brisket sandwich; drizzle over some fresh smoked sausage; or toss in some hot, fatty pulled pork, this sauce will take you ALL the way there. If you have a cold-smoking gun (optional), use it.

½ cup (108g) firmly packed dark brown sugar

1 cup (272g) **ketchup (page 42)**

3 tbsp (63g) molasses

¼ cup (60ml) white distilled vinegar

1 tbsp (10g) garlic powder

1 tbsp (7g) smoked paprika

1½ tsp (4g) cayenne

1 tbsp (15ml) Worcestershire sauce

1 tbsp (18g) kosher salt

1 tsp (3g) freshly cracked black pepper

1 In a medium saucepan, stir together all of the ingredients. Place over medium heat, and let the mixture come to a simmer. Once simmering, continue cooking, stirring occasionally, for 6 to 8 minutes, or until reduced and thickened slightly.

2 Pour the barbecue sauce into a bowl. If you have a smoking gun, cover the bowl with plastic wrap and slide the probe of the gun into the bowl. Fill the bowl with smoke, and remove the probe. Let sit, covered, for 5 minutes. Stir, taste, and repeat 2 or 3 more times until smoky to your liking.

3 Serve how you like it! Store in an airtight container in the refrigerator for up to 1 month.

mayonnaise

We've seen it everywhere on the internet. Oh, the magical mayonnaise gods, please dear gods bless me with a beautiful emulsion and don't strike me down with a clumpy, disgusting mess. Look, nobody here can help you but yourself. Just be patient and observe my go-to method.

1 cup (250ml) neutral-tasting oil
2 large egg yolks
Juice of 2 lemons
1 tbsp (15g) Dijon mustard
Generous pinch of kosher salt, to taste

1 Add the oil to a squirt bottle with a small tip attachment. (This is optional but recommended; otherwise, just pour the oil from a cup.) To a medium bowl, add the egg yolks. Whisk in the lemon juice, mustard, and a pinch of salt.

2 While constantly whisking, gently and slowly squeeze the squirt bottle to add small droplets of oil, one at a time, to the egg yolk mixture. Once the mixture begins to turn a lighter color, you can start to add the oil in a light, steady stream. Continue constantly whisking while maintaining the steady stream of oil.

3 Once all the oil is added and you have an emulsified mayonnaise, you're done! If it is loose and not very thick, the emulsion likely broke and needs to be restabilized (see note). Store in an airtight container in the refrigerator for up to 1 week.

note: Fixing broken mayo is easy, and it begins with you not panicking. Pour the broken mayonnaise into the squirt bottle. To a new medium bowl, add 2 more egg yolks, and whisk in juice from 1 lemon and ½ tablespoon (8g) mustard. While constantly whisking, VERY slowly stream in the entire broken emulsion mixture. If done very slowly, you now have a thick, stable mayonnaise.

PREP TIME:
10 MINUTES

COOK TIME:
20 MINUTES

YIELD:
ABOUT 1½ CUPS

jalapeño salsa

Sure, sure, we all know the classic red salsa. It's usually a medium- or mild-tasting salsa, and, in my opinion, overused. Don't you get tired of that taste? Don't you want something that will take you to a level you never thought possible? Okay, maybe you don't, but chances are you don't because you either don't like spicy food, or you just need to EXPERIENCE the truth. You'll love this smooth, jalapeño-y, garlicky sauce.

1¼ lb (550g) jalapeños
9 cloves garlic (7 cloves thinly sliced and 2 cloves whole), divided
½ cup (125ml) neutral-tasting oil
Juice of 1 lime
Kosher salt, to taste

1 With a blow torch or gas burner, char the jalapeños until all sides are completely charred. As you're working, place the charred jalapeños in a heatproof container, cover, and let steam.

2 In a small pot, add the 7 cloves of sliced garlic. Cover with the oil, set over medium heat, and cook until slightly toasted. Then strain the garlic and oil through a fine-mesh strainer into a small container.

3 Using paper towels, remove the charred skins from the steamed jalapeños. Discard the stems, and place the jalapeños into a blender.

4 To the blender, add the toasted garlic cloves and the remaining 2 raw garlic cloves, along with the juice of 1 lime.

5 Blend on high speed until smooth, adding a splash of water if needed to loosen. Then, while the motor is running on high, slowly stream in the garlic oil until emulsified.

6 Season to taste with salt. Enjoy or store in an airtight container in the refrigerator for up to 2 weeks.

flavored mayos

This isn't so much a list of recipes as it is ideas to get you started on the beautiful, lovely, make-you-wanna-cry-and-sing-on-the-mountaintops world of mayonnaise. It's hands down the most underutilized and underrated condiment in the game. If you don't eat your fries with mayo, it's time to open your mind.

Herby mayo:
1 cup (230g)
  **mayonnaise
  (page 44)**
2 tbsp (6g) finely sliced
  chives
¼ cup (15g) very finely
  chopped flat-leaf
  parsley
2 tsp (3g) finely chopped
  thyme leaves
1 tbsp (15ml) red wine
  vinegar
Kosher salt and freshly
  cracked black pepper,
  to taste

Addicting spicy mayo:
1 cup (230g)
  **mayonnaise
  (page 44)**
2 tsp (5g) smoked
  paprika
1 tbsp (15ml) **hot sauce
  (page 41;** make it
  extra hot)
1 tbsp (15g) chili oil
  solids
3 cloves garlic, grated
3 tbsp (2g) bonito flake
  powder (see notes)
2 tbsp (30ml) fresh
  lemon juice
Kosher salt, to taste

Ultra-garlicky mayo:
1 cup (230g)
  **mayonnaise
  (page 44)**
4 cloves garlic, grated
4 cloves garlic, sautéed
  in oil until toasted
  (see notes)
3 cloves black garlic,
  finely minced
Kosher salt, to taste
1 tbsp (15ml) sherry
  vinegar

Pesto mayo:
1 cup (230g)
  **mayonnaise
  (page 44)**
⅓ cup (75ml) **pesto
  sauce (page 42)**
Kosher salt, to taste
Zest and juice of 1 lemon

1 In a medium bowl, stir together all of the ingredients for your desired mayo flavor until thoroughly combined.

2 Chill. These mayos taste best after sitting and allowing the flavors to marry for at least a few hours and ideally overnight. Store in an airtight container in the refrigerator for up to 1 week.

notes: For the bonito in the addicting spicy mayo, simply place all your bonito flakes into a blender and blend on high speed until you get as close to a powder as possible.

For the toasted garlic in the ultra-garlicky mayo, thinly slice the garlic. Place it in a small skillet, add enough olive oil or neutral-tasting oil to cover, and cook over medium heat until the garlic is golden brown. Once golden, immediately strain before it burns. Let it cool completely. You can save the oil for a different use, such as adding to salad dressing. Use that toasted garlic, and love your life.

ADDICTING
SPICY MAYO

HERBY MAYO

ULTRA-
GARLICKY
MAYO

PREP TIME:
**5 MINUTES +
CHILLING + MAKING
MAYO (IF DESIRED)**

YIELD:
1¾ CUPS

ranch dressing

I find that its flavor is actually best after sitting for at least 24 hours before serving.

¾ cup (173g) **mayonnaise (page 44)**
½ cup (120g) crème fraîche
½ cup (125ml) buttermilk
½ bunch of chives, thinly sliced

3 sprigs dill, finely chopped
½ cup (30g) chopped flat-leaf parsley
1 tbsp (15g) Dijon mustard
3 cloves garlic, grated
Kosher salt and freshly cracked black pepper, to taste

1 In a medium bowl, mix together all of the ingredients except salt and pepper until thoroughly combined. Season to taste with salt and pepper.

2 Use or store in an airtight container in the refrigerator for 7 to 12 days.

PREP TIME:
**10 MINUTES +
MAKING MAYO &
PICKLES (IF DESIRED)**

YIELD:
1½ CUPS

sauce gribiche

Eat with poached fish, roasted potatoes, grilled vegetables...the list goes on.

3 hard-boiled eggs
1 cup (230g) **mayonnaise (page 44)**
1 tbsp (15ml) sherry vinegar
1½ tbsp (23g) Dijon mustard
2 cloves garlic, grated
2 tbsp (24g) finely chopped capers

3 tbsp (29g) finely diced **dill pickles (page 20)**
2 tbsp (6g) thinly sliced chives
3 tbsp (11g) finely chopped flat-leaf parsley
Kosher salt and freshly cracked black pepper, to taste

1 Separate the egg yolks and whites. Press the yolks through a fine-mesh sieve into a small bowl. Very finely dice the whites.

2 In a medium bowl, whisk together the mayonnaise, vinegar, mustard, and garlic. Fold in the capers, pickles, chives, parsley, egg yolks, and egg whites. Season to taste with salt and pepper. Use or store in an airtight container in the refrigerator for up to 2 days.

**RANCH
DRESSING**

**SAUCE
GRIBICHE**

PREP TIME:
5 MINUTES

YIELD:
1½ CUPS

horseradish-chive cream

This sauce was made for the smørrebrød (page 140) until I realized it goes incredibly well with a lot of other foods. I love it folded into mashed potatoes, on top of pork chops, or as a dip for cucumbers or carrots. I'm a big fan of sauces that could solely exist to be delivered to your mouth by hitching a ride on a carrot.

1 cup (240g) crème fraîche
¼ cup (60ml) heavy whipping cream
1 tbsp (15g) freshly grated horseradish

¼ cup (12g) thinly sliced chives
1 clove garlic, grated
Zest of 1 lemon
Kosher salt and freshly cracked black pepper, to taste

1 In a medium bowl, stir together all of the ingredients until well incorporated. Use or store in an airtight container in the refrigerator for 1 week.

PREP TIME:
5 MINUTES + MAKING KETCHUP (IF DESIRED)

YIELD:
¾ CUP

katsu sauce

Katsu sauce is a beautifully simple thing to make, just like many of these sauces. Although it's purpose is literally in the name, you can really use it as an addition to other sauces or simply serve it on just about any meat or vegetable you'd like.

6 tbsp (102g) **ketchup (page 42)**
2 tbsp (30ml) Worcestershire sauce

2 tbsp (40g) oyster sauce
2 tbsp (40g) miso paste (optional)
2 tsp (16g) honey

1 In a small bowl, stir together all of the ingredients until fully incorporated. Use or store in an airtight container in the refrigerator for up to 1 month.

HORSERADISH-CHIVE CREAM

KATSU SAUCE

breads & starches from scratch

This is not a low-carb section, in case you were wondering.

PREP TIME:
**5 MINUTES/DAY FOR
AT LEAST 7 DAYS**

FERMENTATION TIME:
AT LEAST 7 DAYS

YIELD:
1 STARTER

sourdough starter

Ah yes, the number one item that took the internet by storm for years, and still does! This is the breath of life for true bread. There are no packets of yeast and no fancy ingredients—just flour and water. It's a 7-day process, but it only takes 5 minutes a day. If you can brush your teeth, you can definitely keep a sourdough starter alive.

Stone-ground rye flour
Filtered water
Unbleached all-purpose flour (bleached flour won't work)

1 Weigh a glass jar (about ¾ liter/28 fl oz) without the lid, and record the weight in grams.

2 On day 1: Add 100 grams rye flour to the jar, along with 150 grams lukewarm filtered water (85°F/30°C). Vigorously whisk together so all of the flour is hydrated. Cover loosely with the lid; do not screw or clamp it on. Let sit at room temperature for 24 hours.

3 On day 2: Remove enough starter mixture from the jar so 70 grams of the mixture remain in the jar. (You'll need to add 70g to the weight of the jar, which you recorded in step 1, to determine what your vessel should weigh on the scale.) Once you have 70 grams starter remaining in the jar, feed your starter. Add 50 grams rye flour, 50 grams unbleached all-purpose flour, and 115 grams lukewarm filtered water. Stir vigorously until thoroughly combined. Cover loosely and let sit at room temperature for 24 hours.

4 On day 3: Remove all but 70 grams of the starter. Feed the starter with 50 grams rye flour, 50 grams all-purpose flour, and 115 grams lukewarm filtered water. Cover loosely. Let sit at room temperature for 24 hours.

5 On day 4: Remove all but 70 grams of the starter. Feed the starter with 50 grams rye flour, 50 grams all-purpose flour, and 100 grams lukewarm filtered water. Cover loosely. Let sit at room temperature for 24 hours.

The rise and fall of the starter: Yours probably will not look exactly the same as mine, and some days it may seem inactive. Over time, if you feed it at the same time every day, you'll see it rising and falling at similar times day to day.

DAY 1   DAY 2   DAY 3

6 On day 5: Remove all but 70 grams of the starter. Feed the starter with 50 grams rye flour, 50 grams all-purpose flour, and 100 grams lukewarm filtered water. Cover loosely. Let sit at room temperature for 24 hours.

7 On day 6: Remove all but 50 grams of the starter. Feed the starter with 50 grams rye flour, 50 grams all-purpose flour, and 100 grams lukewarm filtered water. Cover loosely. Let sit at room temperature for 24 hours.

8 On day 7: Remove all but 25 grams of the starter. Feed the starter with 50 grams rye flour, 50 grams all-purpose flour, and 100 grams lukewarm filtered water. Cover loosely. Let sit at room temperature for 24 hours. After that time, if the starter is not yet active enough to use (see note), give it a few more days following the day 7 procedure.

9 Once the starter is active, you can continue to feed it so the wild yeast remains active indefinitely. Every day, remove all but 25 grams of starter. (Remember, you can always use the discarded portion to make bread!) Add 50 grams rye flour, 50 grams all-purpose flour, and 100 grams room temperature filtered water. Always keep it loosely covered at room temperature. If you forget one or two feedings, you can resume the normal maintenance schedule until it regains its strength. If you're going on vacation and want to put it to sleep, one method is to refrigerate it so it goes into a dormant state; I recommend an online search about this to learn more.

note: There are many tests to determine if the starter is ready. In my experience, the best indicator of a mature starter is when it rises and falls predictably. If you feed it at the same time daily, you should notice it rises to about the same height each day and falls at a similar hour each day.

DAY 4

DAY 5

DAY 6

DAY 7

PREP TIME:
**24 HOURS (SEE SAMPLE SCHEDULE) +
MAKING THE STARTER**

COOK TIME:
40–50 MINUTES PER LOAF

YIELD:
**2 (10-INCH/25-CM)
LOAVES**

basic sourdough bread

This is where the beauty of bread genuinely begins. It's something so incredibly special, nobody ever believes it only takes flour, water, and salt to make it. Yes, that's right. You're asking "What about the yeast?" The yeast is in your sourdough starter (page 52), which is composed of only flour and water! Sourdough bread is something that anyone can make, within nearly any budget. It brings a tear to my eye. Check out my YouTube video "No Knead Beginner Sourdough Bread" to see a similar process in action.

White rice flour,
    for dusting

Levain:
35g mature **sourdough
    starter (page 52)**
35g whole wheat flour
35g unbleached
    all-purpose flour
70g filtered water,
    room temperature

Autolyze:
804g unbleached bread
    flour
75g whole wheat flour
740g filtered water,
    heated to 90–95°F
    (32–35°C), divided
18g fine sea salt

1 In a pint-sized jar, thoroughly stir together the levain ingredients. Cover loosely with the lid (do not screw or clamp it on), and let rest in a warm area such as a proofer or cold oven with the light on (78–80°F/ 25–27°C) for 5 hours to ferment (mature/ripen) and rise. It's done when the top is flat and it's just beginning to fall.

2 Ninety minutes before the levain is done, start the autolyze (a.k.a. fully hydrated flour). In a large bowl, using your hand, mix together the bread flour and whole wheat flour. Of the 740 grams filtered warm water, reserve 80 grams in a bowl to the side. Add the remaining 660 grams warm water to the flour for the autolyze. Using your hand, mix just until the flour is hydrated and the dough is shaggy but comes together; do not overmix. It will be very sticky. Cover with plastic wrap or a damp towel and let autolyze (rest and hydrate) in a warm area (78–80°F/25–27°C) for the remaining time the levain has, 1 to 1½ hours.

3 Once the levain has matured and the dough has autolyzed, in the bowl with the autolyze dough, pour the levain over top. Add a few splashes of the reserved (now room temperature) water to the mixture. Using your hands, dimple the levain into the dough. Stir together until the levain begins to incorporate into the dough. Then, using the Rhubaud method (page 15), mix for 2 to 3 minutes until the dough starts to become smooth and the levain is incorporated.

4 Turn the dough onto an unfloured surface. Perform some slap-and-folds: pick up some of the dough with your fingertips, letting it stretch, and then slap it back down as you fold it over itself. Do this repeatedly for 3 minutes. It will start to become less sticky and easier to work with. Place it back in the bowl and let rest for 25 minutes in a warm area.

5 Add the sea salt to the reserved water, and stir to dissolve. Pour the water over the dough. Mix the dough and water with your hands until incorporated. (The dough will be very wet; keep mixing until it comes together.) Turn the dough onto an unfloured surface, and perform

note: If you don't have bannetons, you can get away with a large bowl or basket lined with a large kitchen towel, dusted with rice flour.

the slap-and-folds again. Slap-and-fold for 2 to 3 minutes, or until the dough is smooth and begins to catch some air. Place it back in the bowl and let rest in the same warm area, beginning the 3-hour, 45-minute bulk ferment.

6 During the bulk ferment, you will perform 6 sets of stretch-and-folds spaced out by 15 minutes for the first 3 and 30 minutes for the last 3. For each stretch-and-fold, leaving the dough in the bowl, use one hand to hold the bowl and the other hand to pick up the edge of the dough farthest from you. Stretch it up as far as it extends without tearing; then fold it over itself. Turn the bowl, and repeat all around the perimeter of the bowl. Place the dough back in the warm area, covered, for each rest. After the last stretch-and-fold, cover and let the dough rest for the final 1½ hours of the bulk ferment undisturbed. It should rise about 85 percent in total over the bulk ferment.

7 Gently turn the dough onto an unfloured surface. Using a dampened bench scraper and dampened hands, divide the dough into 2 even pieces. Preshape each piece into a loosely shaped ball (a.k.a. boule). Let rest where they are, uncovered, for 20 minutes.

8 Lightly flour the top of each boule. Carefully flip them so the unfloured sides face up. Shape each into a batard. Gently fold the bottom third of the dough up to the middle, then the left third up and over the middle, then the right side up and over the left, and finally fold the top up and over the bottom of the dough. Carefully roll the dough over so the seam side is down and pull lightly toward you to tighten the seam if needed.

9 Carefully place the batards seam-side up in 2 bannetons (woven baskets lined with cloth; see note on page 55) dusted with either rice flour or all-purpose flour. Seal each banneton individually in a plastic bag and refrigerate overnight to proof, 12 to 14 hours.

10 Preheat the lid and base of a cast-iron combo cooker or 7-quart (6.5-liter) round

Dutch oven to 500°F (260°C) for 1 hour. Lightly dust the exposed side of 1 of your loaves with rice flour, and lightly dust the bottom of the preheated combo cooker. Carefully place the dusted loaf into the hot pan, floured-side down. Score the dough lengthwise from the top to the bottom, about ¼ inch (0.5cm) deep at about a 45-degree angle. Place the lid on top. Bake for 20 minutes at 500°F (260°C).

11 Remove the top from the combo cooker and lower the oven temperature to 450°F (230°C). Bake for an additional 20 to 30 minutes, or until the loaf is a deep brown color. (It's okay if there is a little bit of char; it should be very well done.)

12 Remove the bread and cool completely on a wire rack. Give the pot another 15-minute preheat at 500°F (260°C), and repeat to cook the other loaf. Slice and enjoy. Store on the counter loosely wrapped in a kitchen towel for up to 2 days and then in a resealable bag up to 1 day more.

---

sample schedule:

9 a.m.: Mix levain

1 p.m.: Autolyze dough

2 p.m.: Mix dough and levain

2:30 p.m.: Mix in salt and remaining water; bulk ferment start

2:45 p.m.: Stretch-and-fold #1

3:00 p.m.: Stretch-and-fold #2

3:15 p.m.: Stretch-and-fold #3

3:45 p.m.: Stretch-and-fold #4

4:15 p.m.: Stretch-and-fold #5

4:45 p.m.: Stretch-and-fold #6; rest for 1½ more hours

6:15 p.m.: End of bulk ferment; shape dough (including 20-minute final rest) and refrigerate overnight

Next morning: Preheat the oven as guided, and bake!

PREP TIME:
12–24 HOURS + MAKING THE STARTER

COOK TIME:
50–55 MINUTES

YIELD:
1 (14-INCH/35.5-CM) LOAF

big boy miche

This is a favorite of mine. It's a truly shareable bread. It's the kind you see in all the knight-in-shining-armor movies. When you see it on the screen, you just KNOW that's some good shit. Earthy, tart, chewy, and above all, HUGE.

White rice flour, to dust
1 cup ice cubes

Levain:

25g mature **sourdough starter (page 52)**
25g whole wheat flour
25g unbleached all-purpose flour
50g filtered water, room temperature

Autolyze:

471g unbleached bread flour
314g whole wheat flour
589g filtered water, room temperature
16g fine sea salt

1   In a pint-sized jar, thoroughly stir together the levain ingredients. Cover loosely with the lid (do not screw or clamp it on) and let rest in a warm area such as a proofer or cold oven with the light on (78–80°F/ 25–27°C) for 5 hours to ferment (mature/ripen) and rise. It's done when the top is flat and it's just beginning to fall.

2   Ninety minutes before the levain is done, make the autolyze (a.k.a. fully hydrated flour). In a large bowl, using your hand, mix together the bread flour and whole wheat flour. Of the 589 grams filtered water, reserve about 60 grams water in a bowl to the side. Add the remaining 539g water to the flour for the autolyze. Using your hand, mix just until the flour is hydrated and the dough is shaggy but comes together; do not overmix. It will be very sticky. Cover with plastic wrap or a damp towel and let autolyze (rest and hydrate) in a warm area (78–80°F/25–27°C) for the remaining time the levain has, 1 to 1½ hours.

3   Once the levain has matured and the dough has autolyzed, in the bowl with the autolyze dough, pour the levain over top. Add half of the reserved water. Using your hands, dimple the levain into the dough. Stir together until the levain begins to incorporate into the dough. Then, using the Rhubaud method (page 15), mix for 2 to 3 minutes until the dough starts to become smooth and the levain is incorporated. Cover with plastic wrap, and let the dough rest in a warm area for 20 minutes.

4   Add the sea salt to the reserved water, and stir to dissolve. Pour the water over the dough. Mix the dough and water with your hands until incorporated. (The dough will be very wet; keep mixing until it comes together.)

5   Repeat the Rhubaud method again for 3 minutes, or until the dough is smooth and elastic. Cover the bowl with plastic wrap and move to a very warm place (about 80°F/27°C), beginning the 3-hour bulk ferment.

6 During the bulk ferment, you will perform 4 sets of stretch-and-folds spaced out by 15 minutes for the first 2 and 30 minutes for the last 2. For each stretch-and-fold, leaving the dough in the bowl, use one hand to hold the bowl and the other hand to pick up the edge of the dough farthest from you. Stretch it up as far as it extends without tearing; then fold it over itself. Turn the bowl, and repeat all around the perimeter of the bowl. Place the dough back in the warm area, covered, for each rest. After the last stretch-and-fold, cover and let the dough rest for the final 1½ hours of the bulk ferment undisturbed.

7 Lightly flour a surface. Carefully scrape the dough from the bowl with a bowl scraper. Using a dampened bench scraper and dampened hands, gently preshape the dough into a very large loosely shaped ball (a.k.a. boule). Let rest right where it is, uncovered, for 20 minutes.

8 Lightly flour the top of the boule. Carefully flip it so the unfloured side faces up. Gently fold the bottom third of the dough up to the middle, then the left third up and over the middle, then the right side up and over the left, and finally fold the top up and over the bottom of the dough. Flip the dough seam-side down on the surface. Keeping your pinkies in contact with the work surface, gently pull the dough toward you. Quarter turn the dough, and repeat the pulling and turning around the dough until it has medium tension and you've done a full 360-degree revolution.

9 Carefully place the shaped dough seam-side up in a very large wicker basket (banneton; at least 12-inch/30.5-cm in diameter and holds at least 3 lb/1.5kg) that's been dusted with rice flour. Seal the basket in a plastic bag and proof at room temperature for 2 hours, or in the refrigerator overnight (12 to 14 hours).

10 Adjust the oven rack to the lower third of the oven. Place a large pizza stone on the rack. Place a medium roasting pan at the very bottom of the oven. Preheat the oven to 500°F (260°C) for 1 hour.

11 Line a pizza peel with a piece of parchment paper about the size of the pizza stone. Carefully invert the dough onto the center of the paper. Gently flour the top of the dough. With a razor blade or sharp knife, lightly score the dough in a crosshatch pattern.

12 Slide the dough and the parchment paper onto the pizza stone, quickly pour 1 cup of ice cubes into the roasting pan, and using a food-safe spray bottle, spray the walls of the oven with water (not the dough or the stone), to generate steam. Immediately close the door. Bake for 20 minutes with the steam. Then remove the baking pan used for steaming, and bake for an additional 30 to 35 minutes, or until the loaf is deeply browned and the internal temperature is about 206°F (97°C).

13 Cool the loaf completely on a wire rack. This will likely take a couple of hours, or let it sit out overnight to enhance the flavors. Slice and enjoy. Store on the counter loosely wrapped in a kitchen towel or paper bag for up to 2 days and then in a resealable bag for 1 more day. Freeze in an airtight container for up to 2 months.

PREP TIME:
**25 MINUTES + 1½ HOURS TO RISE +
SHAPING + MAKING BUTTER (IF DESIRED)**

COOK TIME:
20 MINUTES

YIELD:
9

my famous multipurpose dough

Let me start off by saying I can't fully take credit for how genius this recipe seems because I sort of created it by accident. Originally, this recipe was developed specifically as a dinner roll, but after a small tweak and some experimentation with elements of other recipes, it turned out that it could be used to make nearly any kind of bun, roll, or simple bread you can think of.

½ cup (125ml) whole milk, heated to about 100°F (38°C)

½ cup (125ml) filtered water, heated to about 100°F (38°C)

2½ tsp (9g) instant dry yeast

3½ cups (525g) unbleached bread flour, plus more for dusting

1 tbsp (13g) granulated sugar

1½ tsp (9g) fine sea salt

1 large egg

1 large egg yolk

2½ tbsp (35g) **unsalted butter (page 33),** softened

Tangzhong:

2 tbsp (18g) unbleached all-purpose flour

2 tbsp (30ml) filtered water

¼ cup (60ml) whole milk

1 Make the tangzhong. In a small saucepan, whisk together the all-purpose flour, water, and milk until completely dissolved. Heat over medium heat, stirring continuously, until the mixture thickens into a thick paste. Transfer to a small bowl, and set aside to cool.

2 In a heatproof bowl, add the warmed milk and water. Stir in the yeast, cover with plastic wrap, and let sit for 10 minutes. The mixture should get lightly foamy, and the yeast should dissolve.

3 In the bowl of a stand mixer, whisk together the bread flour, sugar, and salt until thoroughly combined. Fit the stand mixer with the dough hook. Begin mixing on medium-low speed. One at a time, add the yeast mixture, the whole egg, and the egg yolk. Once the mixture starts to come together, add the tangzhong. Mix for 3 to 4 minutes, or until the dough is smooth and elastic.

4 Add the butter, and continue mixing on medium-low speed for another 2 minutes, or until all of the butter is incorporated and the dough is smooth and supple.

5 Transfer the dough to a large greased bowl, and cover with greased plastic wrap. Let rise at room temperature for 1½ hours, or until the dough has doubled in size.

6 Punch down the dough to release the gas and turn onto a lightly floured surface. Shape and bake as desired according to pages 62 to 63. Store the cooled buns or rolls in a resealable bag on the counter for up to 4 days or in an airtight container in the freezer for up to 2 months.

BREADS & STARCHES FROM SCRATCH

For baking:
1 large egg, beaten

burger & sandwich buns

1 Preheat the oven to 375°F (190°C). Line a baking sheet with parchment paper. Divide the dough into 6 to 9 even pieces, depending on how large you want your buns. Shape each piece into a tight ball by stretching and folding the sides over into the center of the dough. Flip it over so it's seam-side down. Roll the dough ball in circles while maintaining constant contact with the surface until you've formed a tight ball.

2 Arrange the dough balls evenly spaced at least 1 inch (2.5cm) apart on the baking sheet. Brush the buns with the egg to lightly coat each top.

3 Bake for about 15 minutes, or until beautifully golden brown. Remove and let cool slightly on the pan and then transfer the buns to a wire rack to cool completely.

4 In most scenarios, toast immediately before assembling the burgers or sandwiches.

BURGER & SANDWICH BUNS

For baking:
1 large egg, beaten

hot dog buns

1 Line a baking sheet with parchment paper. Divide the dough into 9 even pieces. Shape each piece into a tight ball by stretching and folding the sides over into the center of the dough. Flip it over so it's seam-side down. Roll the dough ball in circles while maintaining constant contact with the work surface until you've formed a tight ball. Cover with a damp towel and let rest for 10 minutes.

2 Using both hands, gently roll 1 of the dough balls into a log about 4½ inches (11.5cm) long. Place the dough log at one end of the baking sheet. Repeat, laying each dough log snugly against the previous one, until all of the logs are lined up in a row. (Yes, they should be touching each other.) Cover with a damp towel and proof for 30 minutes. Once nearly done proofing, preheat the oven to 375°F (190°C).

3 Brush the proofed buns with the egg to lightly coat each top. Bake for 12 to 15 minutes, or until beautifully puffed and golden brown.

4 Without breaking the line of buns, transfer to a wire rack and cool completely. Break the line of buns apart and use as desired.

DINNER ROLLS

HOT DOG BUNS

dinner rolls

1 Lightly grease an 8-inch (20-cm) square baking pan. Divide the dough into 9 even pieces. Shape each piece into a tight ball by stretching and folding the sides over into the center of the dough. Flip it over so it's seam-side down. Roll the dough ball in circles while maintaining constant contact with the work surface until you've formed a tight ball.

2 In the baking pan, arrange the dough balls in rows of 3. Cover with a damp towel and let proof at room temperature for 30 minutes, or until doubled in size. Once nearly done proofing, preheat the oven to 375°F (190°C).

3 Brush the proofed rolls with the egg to lightly coat each top. Bake for 16 to 18 minutes, or until beautifully puffed and golden brown.

4 When they're almost done baking, in a small pot, gently heat the butter over medium heat until melted. Turn off the heat. Add the garlic and gently swirl around for 10 seconds.

5 Remove the rolls from the oven and immediately brush with the garlic butter. Top with a sprinkle of salt. Serve warm from the oven for the best texture and flavor.

For baking:
1 large egg, beaten
⅓ cup (75g) **salted butter (page 33)**
2 cloves garlic, finely chopped
Flaky sea salt, for sprinkling

63

PREP TIME:
**50 MINUTES + 2½ HOURS TO RISE +
MAKING BUTTER (IF DESIRED)**

COOK TIME:
35–40 MINUTES

YIELD:
**1 (9 X 4½-INCH/
23 X 11.5-CM) LOAF**

grocery store white bread

We all know our favorite grocery store white bread. Although I usually prefer sourdough or a loaf of bread with something more interesting to it, I can't help my nostalgia for the strangely soft rectangular loaves from the store.

¾ cup (175ml) filtered water

½ cup (125ml) whole milk

1 pkg (9g) instant dry yeast

3 cups (440g) unbleached bread flour, plus more for dusting

1½ tsp (9g) fine sea salt

1 tbsp (13g) granulated sugar

3 tbsp (42g) **unsalted butter (page 33),** softened, plus more for greasing

1 In a small bowl, combine the water and whole milk, and heat to 100°F (38°C). Stir in the yeast, cover with plastic wrap, and let sit for 10 minutes. The mixture should get lightly foamy, and the yeast should dissolve.

2 In the bowl of a stand mixer, combine the bread flour, salt, and sugar. Whisk until thoroughly combined.

3 Fit the stand mixer with the dough hook. Start mixing on low speed. Slowly add the yeast mixture, and mix until combined, scraping down the sides as needed. Once a cohesive dough is formed, keep mixing for another 2 to 3 minutes, or until smooth.

4 Add the softened butter 1 tablespoon (14g) at a time until each addition is incorporated and then mix for 30 seconds more on low speed. Cover the bowl with plastic wrap, and rest the dough for 10 minutes.

5 After 10 minutes, place the dough on an unfloured surface, and gently shape it into a ball. Place into a large greased bowl and cover with greased plastic wrap. Let rise at room temperature for 1 to 1½ hours, or until doubled in size.

6 Lightly grease a 9 x 4½-inch (23 x 11.5-cm) loaf pan with butter. Punch down the dough to release the gas and place on a lightly floured surface. Using a rolling pin, roll the dough into a ½-inch- (1.25-cm-) thick rectangle, with the short edge about 9 inches (23cm) long. Tightly roll up the dough into a cylinder, starting at the short edge.

7 Place the rolled dough into the greased loaf pan. Cover with a damp towel or another inverted loaf pan and let rise at room temperature for 45 minutes to 1 hour, or until doubled in size. Toward the end of the rise time, preheat the oven to 350°F (180°C).

8 Add the loaf pan to the preheated oven, and bake for 35 to 40 minutes, or until golden brown. Cool for 5 minutes in the pan and then carefully remove from the loaf pan and let cool completely on a wire rack. Store in an airtight container on the counter for up to 4 days or in the freezer for up 1 month.

PREP TIME:
45 MINUTES

COOK TIME:
40 MINUTES

YIELD:
1 (9-INCH/23-CM) LOAF

bagel loaf

It's exactly what it says it is: literally a bagel in the form of a loaf of bread. It's life changing. Use as normal bread, or treat it just like you would a bagel, toasted and spread with some cream cheese and topped with lox.

1 large egg
1 tbsp (15ml) filtered water

Dough:
297g filtered water, heated to 90°F (32°C)
23g granulated sugar
10g instant dry yeast
500g unbleached bread flour, plus more for dusting
6g fine sea salt

Everything seasoning:
2 tbsp (7g) dried garlic flakes
2½ tbsp (9g) dried onion flakes
1½ tbsp (14g) white sesame seeds
1 tbsp (9g) black sesame seeds
1 tbsp (10g) poppy seeds
½ tbsp (9g) flaky sea salt

1   Start the dough. In a small bowl, stir together the warm water, sugar, and yeast. Cover with plastic wrap, and let sit for 10 minutes. The mixture should get lightly foamy, and the yeast should dissolve.

2   In a large bowl, stir together the bread flour and salt. Mix the yeast mixture into the flour mixture by hand until all of the flour is hydrated.

3   Turn the dough onto an unfloured surface and knead for 5 to 6 minutes, or until smooth. To knead, fold the dough in half toward you, pressing down and outward with the heel of your hand. Give the dough a quarter turn and continue folding and pushing with the heel of your hand. Once smooth, place the dough in a lightly greased large bowl, cover with greased plastic wrap, and let rise for 1 hour at room temperature. Before the dough is done rising, preheat the oven to 375°F (190°C) and grease a 9-inch (23-cm) loaf pan.

4   While the dough is rising, prepare the everything seasoning. In a small bowl, mix together all of the ingredients. Once used, store the leftover seasoning in an airtight container.

5   Punch down the dough to release the gas, and turn the dough onto a lightly floured surface. Roll the dough into a 10-inch (25-cm) square, about ½ inch (1.25cm) thick.

6   From the bottom edge of the dough, tightly roll the dough into a cylinder. Place it in the greased loaf pan. Cover with plastic wrap and let rest for 15 minutes. Fill a medium pot (at least 10 inches/25cm) with water deep enough to submerge the dough. Bring to a boil.

7   Carefully remove the dough from the pan and submerge it into the boiling water. Boil for 1 minute, flip, and boil for 1 more minute.

8   Carefully transfer the boiled dough back to the loaf pan. In a small bowl, whisk together the egg and water. Brush the top of the dough with the egg wash. Sprinkle with the desired amount of everything seasoning. Bake for 25 to 35 minutes, or until golden brown. Cool for 5 minutes in the pan and then carefully remove from the pan and let cool completely on a wire rack. Slice and serve. Store in an airtight container on the counter for up to 4 days or in the freezer for up to 1 month.

PREP TIME:
**40 MINUTES + 1½ HOURS TO RISE +
EXTRACTING LARD (IF DESIRED)**

COOK TIME:
28–32 MINUTES

YIELD:
2 (16-INCH/40-CM) LOAVES

cubano bread

The beauty of this water-misted, almost baguette-like bread is that it leads to something even greater than the sum of its parts—the coveted Cubanos (page 178).

1¼ cups (310ml) filtered water, heated to 100°F (38°C)

1 tbsp (10g) instant dry yeast

3½ cups (500g) unbleached bread flour, plus more for dusting

1 tbsp (13g) granulated sugar

2 tsp (12g) fine sea salt

2½ tbsp (30g) lard (see **extracted animal fat, page 32**), solidified

1 In a small bowl, stir together the warm water and yeast. Cover with plastic wrap, and let sit for 10 minutes. The mixture should get lightly foamy, and the yeast should dissolve.

2 To the bowl of a stand mixer, add the bread flour, sugar, and salt. Whisk together until thoroughly combined. Fit the stand mixer with the dough hook. Start mixing on medium-low speed. Slowly add the warm yeast mixture and the lard. Mix until combined. Once a cohesive dough is formed, keep mixing for another 3 to 5 minutes, or until smooth.

3 Shape the dough into a ball, and place in a greased medium bowl covered with greased plastic wrap. Let rise at room temperature for 45 minutes to 1 hour, or until doubled in size.

4 Punch down the dough to release the gas and place on a lightly floured surface. Divide the dough into 2 even pieces. Cover with a damp towel, and let them rest right where they are for 10 minutes.

5 Flatten out 1 piece of dough into about a ½-inch- (1.25-cm-) thick rectangle, with the long edge about 10 inches (25cm) long. From the long edge, tightly roll the dough and close the seams at the bottom and sides.

6 Carefully roll the log while applying pressure outward to slightly taper the ends. The log should be 16 inches (40cm) long. Repeat with the other piece of dough.

7 Place the loaves onto a parchment-lined baking sheet 4 to 6 inches (10–15.25cm) apart. Cover with another baking sheet. Let the dough proof for about 30 minutes at room temperature.

8 About 10 minutes before the dough is done proofing, bring a 10-inch (25-cm) ovenproof skillet of water to a boil. Preheat the oven to 400°F (200°C). Remove the top baking sheet. Using a food-safe spray bottle, lightly spray the dough with water. Using a razor blade or an extremely sharp knife, score a shallow seam along the length of the loaves.

9 Place the skillet of boiling water on the bottom rack of the oven. Place the baking sheet with the dough in the middle of the oven on a separate rack above the water. Spray the inside of the oven with a little water to generate steam.

10 Let the bread steam for 8 to 10 minutes. Reduce the heat to 375°F (190°C), remove the skillet of water, and let the bread bake for another 20 to 22 minutes, or until lightly browned.

11 Let cool completely on a wire rack. Slice and serve. Store on the counter loosely wrapped in a kitchen towel for up to 2 days and then in a resealable bag for 1 more day. Freeze in an airtight container for up to 2 months.

note: Make these loaves a day or two ahead of time if you will be toasting the slices.

fresh pasta

Let me be very honest with you. Making your own pasta is superior, but not necessarily because of just taste and texture. What it really gives you is control over arguably one of the world's most favorite foods. That means any shape, any style of pasta, wherever you are, whenever you want (...to a certain extent depending on your equipment).

3 cups (450g) 00 flour or unbleached all-purpose flour, plus more for dusting
½ tsp (3g) fine sea salt
5 large eggs
1 tsp (5ml) extra-virgin olive oil

1 On a flat surface or in a bowl, form a mound of the flour and sprinkle the salt over the top. With your hand (formed in a clawlike shape), make a well in the middle of the flour mound that is large enough to hold the eggs. Crack the eggs into the well, and drizzle the olive oil over the eggs. Using a fork, begin gently whisking the eggs and oil until mixed together. Once the eggs come together, continue whisking while slowly bringing in some of the flour; be careful not to make a path for the eggs to flow out.

2 Once the mixture begins to develop clumps and eventually forms into a dough, begin using your hands to mix and squeeze until fully combined. If the dough is too dry, add water 1 tablespoon (15ml) at a time until it comes together. If using a bowl, turn the dough onto a lightly floured surface. Knead the dough for 5 to 7 minutes, or until smooth. To knead, fold the dough in half toward you, and press down and outward with the heel of your hand. Give the dough a quarter turn, and continue folding and pushing with the heel of your hand. Wrap in plastic wrap, and refrigerate for at least 1 hour or overnight.

3 To shape, place the chilled dough on a lightly floured surface. Cut the dough into 3 or 4 sections, and work with 1 section at a time while keeping the rest covered.

4 To machine shape the pasta (recommended), run the sections through the machine to flatten according to the manufacturer's instructions until thin enough to see your hand through. Cut the long sheets of dough into about 8-inch- (20-cm-) long rectangles. Run the sections through the desired ribbon attachment to cut.

5 To hand shape the pasta, dust each side of the section with flour, and use a rolling pin to roll into a long, thin rectangle, pausing to release it from the counter as needed. Cut the sheet of dough into about 8-inch- (20-cm-) long rectangles. Starting with the short edge, fold the rectangles into flat, rectangular rolls. Using a very sharp knife, cut at regular intervals for the desired width of ribbon (about ½ inch/1.25cm for tagliatelle, and about 1 inch/2.5cm for pappardelle). I don't recommend cutting narrower shapes, such as spaghetti, by hand. Unfurl the ribbons.

6 To cook, add the ribbons to salted boiling water, and cook for 1 to 3 minutes, or until al dente.

Kneading dough (step 2)

Machine-shaped pasta (step 4)

Hand-shaped pasta (step 5)

potato gnocchi

Gnocchi is hands down one of the easiest "pasta dumplings" to make completely from scratch. It comes together very quickly, especially if you have any leftover baked potatoes. (But if I'm being honest, who just has leftover baked potatoes f—ing hanging out in the refrigerator?) I guess what I'm trying to say is gnocchi is your best bet for a high success rate on your first pasta. (Although technically this is a dumpling.)

2 lb (1kg) russet potatoes
1 large egg, whisked
2 cups (300g) unbleached all-purpose flour, plus more for dusting
1 tsp (6g) fine sea salt

1 Add the potatoes to a large pot, and just cover with water. Bring to a boil over medium-high heat. Cover and cook for about 30 minutes, or until the potatoes are easily pierced with a fork.

2 Drain the potatoes and let them sit just until cool enough to handle, about 10 minutes. Discard the skins. Press all the potatoes through a potato ricer or mash with a hand masher until as smooth as possible. Once the potatoes are completely cool, mix the egg into the potatoes.

3 In a medium bowl, whisk together the flour and salt. Mix half of the flour mixture into the potato mixture, and as soon as it starts to combine, add the remaining flour mixture. Turn the dough onto a lightly floured surface. Begin folding and kneading until you get a cohesive dough. Continue kneading the dough for about 3 minutes, or until smooth, dusting the surface lightly with flour if needed.

4 To shape, dust the dough with flour and cut into 5 or 6 equal pieces. Roll each piece of dough into a long cylinder about ½ inch (1.25cm) thick. Cut that cylinder into segments about 1 inch (2.5cm) long. Repeat with the remaining pieces of dough.

5 Once your gnocchi has been cut into pillows, you can leave them as is, but if you want them to hold as much sauce as possible, you should give them ridges. Gently press and roll each pillow along the ridges of a gnocchi roller or the tines of a fork.

6 To cook, add the gnocchi to heavily salted boiling water. Let them cook for a few minutes. The moment they float, they're done. Remove them with a slotted spoon or kitchen spider. See pesto gnocchi (page 173) for my favorite way to sauce these!

POTATO
GNOCCHI

SPAGHETTI

TAGLIATELLE

PREP TIME:
**30 MINUTES + MAKING
BUTTER (IF DESIRED)**

COOK TIME:
17 MINUTES

YIELD:
8

buttermilk biscuits

Fresh buttermilk biscuits. The mere words sound like some sort of slogan you hear in an advertisement for a dairy farm...let these biscuits take you there.

2¾ cups (413g) unbleached all-purpose flour, plus more for dusting

2 tbsp (26g) baking powder

1 tsp (6g) fine sea salt

1 tsp (4g) granulated sugar

⅔ cup (149g) **unsalted butter (page 33),** chilled

1 cup (250ml) buttermilk, plus more for brushing

1 Preheat the oven to 425°F (220°C). Line a baking sheet with parchment paper. In the bowl of a food processor, add the all-purpose flour, baking powder, salt, and sugar, and pulse a few times until thoroughly combined.

2 Cut the butter into ½-inch (1.25-cm) cubes. Make sure the butter is extremely cold. If not, freeze for 5 minutes.

3 Add the butter to the food processor, and pulse 12 to 14 times, or until pea-sized crumbs are formed.

4 Transfer to a medium bowl. While slowly streaming in the buttermilk, use a fork to mix until all of the buttermilk has been poured in and a solid mass has formed. If it's still too dry, add 1 or 2 more tablespoons (15 or 30ml) buttermilk.

5 Turn the dough onto an unfloured surface and gently knead until it comes together. Roll it out into a rough rectangle. Fold it in thirds (like folding a letter) and then roll it out lengthwise. Fold it into thirds again, cover with plastic wrap, and refrigerate for 5 minutes.

6 After resting, place on a lightly floured surface and roll it out into a rectangle about ¾ inch (2cm) thick.

7 Using a 3- to 4-inch (7.5–10-cm) biscuit cutter, cut out as many pieces as possible and place on the baking sheet. Continue to reroll and cut the dough to get as many biscuits as possible.

8 Brush the tops very lightly with buttermilk. Bake for 15 to 17 minutes, or until the tops are golden brown. Split in half, and enjoy!

PREP TIME:
**35 MINUTES + 2 HOURS TO RISE +
MAKING BUTTER (IF DESIRED)**

COOK TIME:
25 MINUTES

YIELD:
9–13

english muffins

Remember when I said we make everything from scratch? I meant everything.

½ cup plus 2 tbsp (139g) filtered water

½ cup plus 2 tbsp (139g) whole milk

1 tbsp (9g) instant dry yeast

4 cups (600g) unbleached bread flour

1 tsp (6g) fine sea salt

1 tbsp (13g) granulated sugar

2 tbsp (28g) **unsalted butter (page 33),** melted and cooled, or neutral-tasting oil

Cornmeal or unbleached all-purpose flour, to dust

1 In a small bowl, combine the water and whole milk, and heat to 100°F (38°C). Stir in the yeast, cover with plastic wrap, and let sit for 10 minutes. The mixture should get lightly foamy, and the yeast should dissolve.

2 In a medium bowl, whisk together the bread flour, salt, and sugar. Add the yeast mixture to the flour mixture, along with the butter. Gently mix with your hands until a shaggy dough is formed.

3 Turn the dough onto an unfloured surface, and knead for 5 to 10 minutes, or until the dough is smooth and shiny.

4 Roll the dough into a ball and place into a greased medium bowl. Cover with a damp towel and let rise at room temperature for 1 hour.

5 Once doubled in size, punch down the dough to release the gas. Place the dough on a lightly floured surface, and lightly flour the top. Using a rolling pin, roll the dough out until about ½ inch (1.25cm) thick.

6 Using a 3-inch (7.5-cm) biscuit cutter, cut out as many rounds as you can. Reroll and form more rounds if possible.

7 Generously dust a baking sheet with cornmeal, and place the rounds onto the sheet. Dust the rounds lightly with more cornmeal. Cover with an inverted baking sheet of the same size or with a damp towel. Let rise at room temperature for 30 minutes to 1 hour, or until puffed up.

8 Lightly grease a cast-iron skillet, griddle pan, or nonstick skillet, and preheat over medium heat. Lightly dust the rounds once more with cornmeal. Once hot, arrange as many rounds as you can fit in the skillet, spacing them about ½ inch (1.25cm) apart. Cook for 5 to 7 minutes, or until lightly browned on the bottom, adjusting the heat as necessary if they brown too quickly. Flip and brown the other side. Place on a wire rack to cool, and repeat with any remaining rounds. Slice in half, and enjoy! Store in an airtight container on the counter for up to 4 days or in the refrigerator for up to 1 week.

PREP TIME:
45 MINUTES

COOK TIME:
6 MINUTES

YIELD:
6–12

flour tortillas

There is no bagged or store-bought tortilla on the entire planet that is anywhere near as perfect as these homemade tortillas. Tortillas lose a majority of their texture and flavor after they cool completely and sit. There is a reason some of the best family-owned taquerias make all of their tortillas (corn or flour) to order.

2 cups (300g) unbleached all-purpose flour, plus more for dusting
1 tsp (6g) kosher salt
½ tsp (2g) baking powder
¾ cup (175ml) filtered water, warm
¼ cup (60ml) neutral-tasting oil

1 In a large bowl, whisk together the all-purpose flour, salt, and baking powder until thoroughly combined.

2 While mixing with a spoon, pour in the warm water, immediately followed by the oil. Mix until it comes together as a ball of dough.

3 Turn the dough onto an unfloured surface, and knead for about 3 minutes, or until it comes together as a smooth ball of dough.

4 Cover with a damp towel, and let rest at room temperature for 30 minutes.

5 Divide the dough into 6 even pieces for burrito-sized tortillas or up to 12 pieces for taco-sized. Roll each piece into a ball.

6 On a lightly floured surface, gently roll each ball of dough to form a 10- to 12-inch (25–30.5-cm) circle.

7 Preheat a 12-inch (20.5-cm) cast-iron skillet over medium-high heat until very hot. Working 1 tortilla at a time, gently lay the tortilla in the skillet and cook for 15 to 30 seconds, or until the bottom becomes lightly charred. Flip and cook until lightly charred on the other side.

8 Remove from the pan and place between a folded towel until ready to serve. Repeat to cook the remaining tortillas. Enjoy!

PREP TIME:
10 MINUTES + MAKING BUTTER (IF DESIRED)

COOK TIME:
35 MINUTES

SERVES:
8

browned butter cornbread

There are two kinds of people: people who think about cornbread, and people who've never had it before.

½ cup (112g) **unsalted butter (page 33)**
½ bunch of sage
½ bunch of thyme
1¼ cups (188g) unbleached all-purpose flour
⅓ cup (67g) granulated sugar
3½ tbsp (47g) light brown sugar
1¼ tsp (8g) fine sea salt
1 tbsp (13g) baking powder
1¼ cups (175g) finely ground yellow cornmeal
2 large eggs
1½ cups (350ml) buttermilk

1 Place an 8-inch (20-cm) cast-iron skillet in a cold oven, and preheat the oven to 400°F (200°C).

2 In a small pot, melt the butter over medium heat. Once melted, continue cooking to brown the butter until it turns dark brown. Then turn off the heat.

3 Add the sage and thyme. Stir to combine, transfer the butter-herb mixture to a separate container, and set aside to cool.

4 In a medium bowl, whisk together the all-purpose flour, granulated sugar, brown sugar, salt, baking powder, and cornmeal.

5 In a separate medium bowl, whisk the eggs. Whisk in the buttermilk.

6 Discard the herbs from the slightly cooled butter. In a slow stream, whisk the butter into the buttermilk mixture. Then whisk the wet mixture into the dry mixture until completely smooth and combined.

7 Remove the hot cast-iron pan from the oven, and lightly grease it with cooking spray. Add the batter to the pan, and spread it evenly.

8 Bake for 20 to 25 minutes, or until a toothpick inserted into the center comes out clean. Cool for a few minutes in the pan and then remove to a cooling rack to cool completely. Cut into 8 wedges, and enjoy!

PREP TIME:
25 MINUTES

COOK TIME:
8–12 MINUTES

YIELD:
24–30

ladyfingers

People always make fun of me for making everything from scratch. This is a perfect example where most people might push back and say this is a waste of time when you can just buy ladyfingers at the store for dishes like tiramisu. Although the time factor is true, the flavor of these beauties, and pride you'll feel when you take them out of the oven, will forever be unmatched.

3 large eggs
½ cup (100g) granulated
   sugar
1 tsp (3g) pure vanilla
   extract
1 cup (150g) unbleached
   all-purpose flour
Small pinch of fine
   sea salt
Powdered sugar, to dust

1 To the bowl of a stand mixer, add the eggs and sugar. Bring a shallow pot of water to a simmer over medium-high heat, and set the stand mixer bowl on top. Make sure the bowl doesn't touch the water.

2 Continuously whisk the eggs and the sugar until the mixture reaches 160°F (70°C). This should take less than 5 minutes. If it curdles, it has overheated, and you should start again.

3 Preheat the oven to 350°F (180°C). Fit the stand mixer with the whisk attachment, and beat the heated egg mixture on high speed for 7 to 10 minutes, or until it's about 2½ times bigger in volume and forms soft peaks.

4 Beat in the vanilla. Remove the bowl from the stand mixer, and gently fold in the all-purpose flour and salt, being careful not to release the air.

5 Line 2 baking sheets with parchment paper, and transfer the batter to a piping bag. Pipe the batter onto the prepared sheets, making them about 3 inches (7.5cm) long and 1 inch (2.5cm) wide, and leaving about 1 inch (2.5cm) space between each ladyfinger.

6 Just before placing the trays in the oven, generously dust the ladyfingers with powdered sugar. Bake both trays at the same time for 8 to 12 minutes, or until lightly golden and crisp.

7 Remove from the trays and place on a wire rack to cool at room temperature. Store in an airtight container at room temperature for up to 3 weeks.

PREP TIME:
15 MINUTES + 1 HOUR TO CHILL

COOK TIME:
15–20 MINUTES

YIELD:
10–12 LARGE CRACKERS

graham crackers

Making your own graham crackers is an instant ego boost, and also an even bigger flavor boost.

¾ cup (112g) unbleached all-purpose flour, plus more for dusting

1½ cups (211g) whole wheat flour

¼ cup (54g) firmly packed dark brown sugar

½ tsp (3g) fine sea salt

1 tsp (4g) baking powder

1½ tsp (4g) ground cinnamon

1 large egg

3½ tbsp (50ml) whole milk, plus more if needed

¼ cup (80g) honey

3 tbsp (45ml) neutral-tasting oil or extra-virgin olive oil

1 In a large bowl, whisk together the all-purpose flour, whole wheat flour, brown sugar, salt, baking powder, and cinnamon until combined.

2 In a medium bowl, whisk the egg. Whisk in the milk, honey, and oil.

3 Add the egg mixture to the flour mixture, and stir. Turn the dough onto an unfloured surface. Knead until a cohesive dough forms. If the dough is too dry, add a splash of milk. Knead until the dough is smooth.

4 Once the dough is smooth, wrap in plastic wrap and refrigerate for 30 minutes to 1 hour.

5 Preheat the oven to 350°F (180°C). Place the dough on a lightly floured surface. Roll into a rough rectangle about ⅛ inch (3mm) thick. Cut the dough into the desired shapes.

6 Place the cut dough on a parchment-lined baking sheet. Using the tines of a fork, poke holes all over the dough. Bake for 15 to 20 minutes, or until the crackers are dry and lightly browned.

7 Cool completely on a wire rack—they will get crispy as they cool. Store in an airtight container at room temperature for up to 1 week.

foundations
applied

This is where you take all the things you learned, made, and got hyped up about in the previous chapters and make life a wonderland...a flavor wonderland, if you will.

breakfast

I'd love to say that we went above and beyond to make things without eggs, except I love eggs for breakfast. These eggs just won't disappoint you.

perfect soft-boiled eggs

There was a point during the infancy of social media when people were putting a sunny-side up fried egg on literally everything. It's delicious, but the idea of it has unfortunately been ruined by the internet (like many things). With that said, I do have a saving grace for you, and that is the humble soft-boiled egg. It's great on its own, on top of some avocado toast (page 124), or floating in a bowl of ramen (page 226).

4 eggs

1 Fill a medium saucepan with enough water to fully submerge the eggs. Bring to a boil over medium-high heat. (Do not add the eggs yet.) Once boiling, slightly lower the temperature so the boil is more gentle but not a simmer.

2 Using a slotted spoon, carefully lower the eggs into the gently boiling water. Cook, uncovered, for exactly 7 minutes.

3 While the eggs are boiling, prepare an ice water bath, filling a medium bowl with equal parts ice and water.

4 As soon as the timer goes off, immediately remove the eggs from the hot water and submerge them in the ice water bath. Let them cool just until room temperature. Peel and enjoy immediately, or refrigerate in the shells for up to 3 days.

BREAKFAST

COOK TIME:
10 MINUTES + MAKING BUTTER (IF DESIRED)

YIELD:
2–3

browned butter–basted fried eggs

Seasoned cooks might think this recipe trivial, but I would ask those same people to reevaluate how incredibly good a perfectly cooked egg with browned butter is. You almost want to eat it completely by itself every time.

2 tbsp (30ml) neutral-tasting oil

2–3 eggs

3 tbsp (42g) **unsalted butter (page 33)**

Freshly cracked black pepper (optional)

Flaky sea salt (such as Maldon or Jacobsen)

1 In a medium skillet, heat the oil over medium-high heat until shimmering and hot.

2 Carefully crack the eggs into the pan, spacing them far enough apart to avoid them forming together. Let the eggs cook, undisturbed, for about 1 minute, or until the whites are mostly set but the yolk is still raw and is still holding onto some raw egg white.

3 Reduce the heat to medium, and add the butter. Let the butter melt completely and froth up. Once melted and frothy, increase the heat to medium-high.

4 Continuously spoon the hot butter over the eggs to baste them until the tops of the eggs are just barely cooked and the yolks are still runny. Carefully remove the eggs from the pan.

5 There should be a couple of tablespoons of browned butter left in the pan. If it's not yet browned, reduce the heat to medium, and cook the butter until it reaches a rich brown color.

6 Spoon the browned butter onto the eggs, and finish with pepper (if using) and salt. Enjoy!

breakfast sandwiches

If you're not familiar with Eggslut, it's an incredible restaurant that serves one of my favorite breakfast sandwiches ever. This is inspired by that sandwich. Alvin, if you're reading, love you, my man.

6 large eggs

4 tbsp (56g) **unsalted butter (page 33),** divided, plus more to toast

1 tbsp (15g) crème fraîche

Kosher salt and freshly cracked black pepper, to taste

½ bunch of chives, thinly sliced

4 sandwich buns (see **my famous multipurpose dough, pages 60–63)**

Ultra-garlicky mayo (page 46), to spread

8 slices cooked bacon

8 slices cheddar or Gouda cheese

1 In a medium saucepan, bring 1 inch (2.5cm) of water to a gentle simmer over medium heat. Place a heatproof bowl on top of the pot, making sure the bowl does not touch the water.

2 Crack the eggs into the bowl, along with 2 tablespoons (28g) butter. Cook, constantly whisking, for 8 to 10 minutes, or until the eggs are cooked and starting to finely curd and come together. Remove from the heat while still creamy and soft.

3 Whisk in the remaining 2 tablespoons (28g) butter, along with the crème fraîche, until melted and well distributed. Season to taste with salt and pepper. Fold in the chives.

4 Toast the buns in a pan with butter until golden brown on the cut sides. To assemble each sandwich, spread ultra-garlicky mayo on the bottom buns. Then add 2 slices of bacon, followed by a generous mound of scrambled egg, and finally 2 slices of cheese. Torch or broil to melt the cheese. Top with your other half of the bun, and enjoy immediately.

PREP TIME:
**10 MINUTES + MAKING MUFFINS
& BUTTER (IF DESIRED)**

COOK TIME:
20 MINUTES

SERVES:
2–4

eggs benedict

Let's not go too far off the beaten path here. This is a hotel banquet classic. Everyone should know how to poach an egg. It can be intimidating, but like many things, you just gotta commit to the movement; don't be timid. I'll make it easy on you with a simple blender-style hollandaise.

Splash of white distilled
 vinegar
4 large eggs
2 tbsp (30ml) extra-virgin
 olive oil
4 slices Canadian bacon
2 **English muffins
 (page 77),** toasted
Cayenne (optional),
 for sprinkling
¼ cup (12g) very thinly
 sliced chives
Freshly cracked black
 pepper, to taste

Hollandaise:
½ cup (112g) **salted
 butter (page 33)**
3 large egg yolks
1 tbsp (15ml) fresh
 lemon juice, plus more
 if needed
½ tsp (1g) cayenne
Kosher salt, to taste

1 Make the hollandaise. In a small saucepan, gently heat the butter over low heat until it's just melted and then remove from the heat. (We don't want it ripping hot—just melted.)

2 To a high-powered blender, add the egg yolks and lemon juice. Blend on high speed until the yolks begin to thicken slightly and turn a lighter color.

3 While blending on high speed, slowly stream in the melted butter. Start with a few drops of butter at first, and work your way up to a solid stream. Once you've streamed in all the butter, you should have a thick and emulsified hollandaise sauce. If it's too thick, just blend in lemon juice a little bit at a time until it's the desired consistency. Add the cayenne, and season to taste with salt. Keep warm, and set aside.

4 Make the poached eggs. Bring a medium saucepan of water to a very gentle boil over medium heat. Add a splash of vinegar to the boiling water. Once it's gently boiling, crack an egg into a ramekin. Using a spoon, swirl the boiling water around in a circular motion in one direction to create a whirlpool. Carefully pour the egg into the center of that whirlpool and let the white naturally wrap around itself. Let it settle in the gently simmering water and cook undisturbed for 3 minutes, or until the white is cooked but the yolk is still runny. Remove from the water with a slotted spoon, and place on a paper towel to drain. Repeat with the rest of the eggs, cooking one at a time.

5 While the eggs are cooking, in a separate pan or on a griddle, heat the olive oil over medium-high heat until ripping hot. Add the Canadian bacon, and sear for 2 minutes on each side, or until nicely browned.

6 To assemble each serving, place a toasted English muffin half on a serving plate. Top with a slice of Canadian bacon and 1 poached egg, and drizzle on the desired amount of hollandaise. Top with cayenne (if using), chives, and pepper to taste. Enjoy!

cinnamon toast

This is one of the biggest throwbacks of my entire childhood—really one of those clichés that my mom used to make me as a kid. But this stuff is...for lack of a better term...a perfect food. Thank you, Mom, for all the times you made this for me. It made bad days turn into great days and taught me the power of a simple recipe, and I still crave it to this day! This makes a big batch of cinnamon-sugar for you to keep in your pantry to use when you need it.

4 thick slices sandwich-style bread (such as **grocery store white bread, page 64, basic sourdough bread, page 54,** or brioche; see notes)

6 tbsp (84g) **salted butter (page 33),** softened

Cinnamon-sugar:
¾ cup (150g) granulated sugar
½ cup (108g) firmly packed light brown sugar
1½ tbsp (12g) ground cinnamon
¼ tsp (0.5g) freshly grated nutmeg (optional)

1 Make the cinnamon-sugar. In a small airtight container or jar, thoroughly mix the granulated sugar, brown sugar, cinnamon, and nutmeg (if using). This will keep for a very long time in the pantry.

2 Toast the bread in a toaster to your desired color. Immediately butter with 1½ tablespoons (21g) butter per slice.

3 Before the butter completely melts, sprinkle generously with cinnamon-sugar. Slice on the diagonal. Enjoy and savor every single nostalgic bite while hot.

notes: I recommend using a whole, unsliced loaf for this and slicing the bread yourself so you can get nice, thick slices.

To change up the flavors, you can first brown the butter and then brush it on, or you can add a dollop of whipped mascarpone on top of each slice of toast.

PREP TIME:
**5 MINUTES +
MAKING BROTH &
DESIRED TOPPINGS**

COOK TIME:
1–1½ HOURS

SERVES:
4–6

congee

I used to make this for myself as a kid after I searched for an alternative to oatmeal and realized savory porridges are a thing. What really showed me the proper way to make it was working all those mornings at Uchiko. If I wasn't making breakfast for the crew that morning, the head pastry chef, Ariana Quant, was making delicious congee like this with all the lovely toppings.

¾ cup (170g) sushi rice
6 cups (1.5 liters) chicken or beef stock (see **basic stock out of anything, page 28**) or **dashi (page 31)**
Kosher salt, to taste

Options for topping:
Thinly sliced green onion
Finely chopped garlic
Chili oil
Soy sauce
Toasted sesame oil
Toasted sesame seeds
Perfect soft-boiled eggs (page 90)
Roasted meat (such as **roasted chicken, page 162**)

1 Thoroughly rinse the rice and add to a medium pot.

2 Add the chicken stock. Bring to a gentle simmer over medium heat, slightly reducing the heat as needed to maintain a gentle simmer. Simmer for 1 to 1½ hours, stirring every 15 minutes, until the rice thickens and breaks.

3 Ladle the hot congee into serving bowls. Lightly season the servings with salt to taste. Enjoy with the desired toppings.

PREP TIME:
**50 MINUTES + ABOUT
3 HOURS TO RISE + MAKING
BUTTER (IF DESIRED)**

COOK TIME:
30 MINUTES

YIELD:
1 DOZEN

hokkaido milk bread cinnamon rolls

When you bite into that tender, spiraled cinnamon-scented bread, it doesn't matter who you are, where you're from, or whether you cook or not...you know you're eating a beautifully made cinnamon roll. The nearly commercial-level fluffiness of the rolls is achieved by using something called a tangzhong. To put it simply, it's basically a roux of precooked flour that helps add spring and lightness to the final dough.

Tangzhong:
- 2 tbsp (18g) unbleached all-purpose flour
- 2 tbsp (30ml) filtered water
- ¼ cup (60ml) whole milk

Dough:
- 1 cup (250ml) whole milk, heated to about 98°F (37°C)
- 2¼ tsp (7g) instant dry yeast
- 4 cups (600g) unbleached all-purpose flour, plus more for dusting
- ½ cup (100g) granulated sugar
- ¾ tsp (5g) fine sea salt
- 2 large eggs
- 1 large egg yolk
- 4 tbsp (56g) **unsalted butter (page 33),** softened
- 2 tbsp (30ml) neutral-tasting oil

Filling:
- $^1/_3$ cup (75g) **unsalted butter (page 33),** softened
- 1 cup (215g) firmly packed dark brown sugar
- 2 tbsp (24g) muscovado sugar
- 2½ tbsp (17g) ground cinnamon

Glaze:
- 4 oz (110g) cream cheese, softened
- 1 cup (125g) powdered sugar
- 2 tsp (10ml) pure vanilla extract
- 2½ tbsp (40ml) whole milk

1 Make the tangzhong. In a small saucepan, whisk together the flour, water, and milk until completely dissolved. Heat over medium heat, stirring continuously, until the mixture thickens into a thick paste. Transfer to a small bowl, and set aside to cool.

2 Start the dough. In a small bowl, add the milk. Stir in the yeast, cover with plastic wrap, and let sit for 10 minutes. The mixture should get lightly foamy, and the yeast should dissolve.

3 In the bowl of a stand mixer, whisk together the flour, sugar, and salt. Fit the mixer with the dough hook, and begin mixing the dry ingredients on medium-low speed. While the motor is running, one at a time, add the yeast mixture, the thickened and fully cooled tangzhong, the eggs (one egg at a time), and finally the egg yolk. Continue mixing on medium-low speed for 3 to 5 minutes, or until the dough is smooth and elastic.

4 Increase the speed to medium, and mix in the butter 1 tablespoon (14g) at a time, allowing each addition to fully incorporate before adding the next. Add the oil 1 tablespoon (15ml) at a time in the same way. The dough will slide around a bit, so turn the machine off as needed to scrape down the sides as you mix until all of the oil is incorporated and you have a smooth, lovely dough.

5 Remove the dough from the bowl, and gently shape it into a loose ball. Lightly grease a medium bowl with cooking spray, and add the dough. Cover with greased plastic wrap. Allow to rise for 1 to 2 hours at room temperature, or until doubled in size. Grease a 9 x 13-inch (23 x 33-cm) baking dish with cooking oil, and set aside.

6 Punch down the dough to release the gas and turn onto a lightly floured surface. Dust the dough with flour and roll into a 13-inch- (33-cm-) long rectangle about ¼ inch (0.5cm) thick.

7 For the filling, brush the entire surface with the softened butter. In a small bowl, stir together the brown sugar, muscovado sugar, and cinnamon until thoroughly combined. Sprinkle all of the cinnamon-sugar mixture evenly across the entire surface of the dough.

8 From the long edge, roll the dough into a lovely 13-inch- (33-cm-) long log. Using a serrated knife, cut the dough into 12 equally sized rounds.

9 Arrange the rounds in the baking dish. Cover the dish with a damp towel and let proof at room temperature for 35 to 45 minutes. Once nearly done rising, preheat the oven to 375°F (190°C).

HOKKAIDO MILK BREAD CINNAMON ROLLS

10 Bake the cinnamon rolls for 15 to 20 minutes, or until the dough is golden brown.

11 While the rolls are baking, prepare the glaze. In a medium bowl, using a handheld mixer or whisk, beat the cream cheese until creamy and smooth. Then beat in the powdered sugar until you get a shaggy paste. Add the vanilla and whole milk, and whisk together until you get a nice drizzly consistency. Add more milk if the glaze is too thick.

12 Let the rolls cool for about 8 minutes and then drizzle all of the glaze over the top. Enjoy while still warm.

PREP TIME:
10 MINUTES + MAKING BREAD & BUTTER (IF DESIRED)

COOK TIME:
5–10 MINUTES

SERVES:
2

french toast

This one of those foods you rarely see people making at home for some reason—it's an "order at brunch" kind of thing. But the irony is that really all you need to do is dip a slice of bread in a milk-egg mixture and toast it. You have complete control over the flavor and texture, which is a big advantage to making your perfect French toast.

3 large eggs
3 large egg yolks
1 tsp (3g) ground cinnamon
¼ tsp (0.5g) freshly grated nutmeg
2 tbsp (26g) granulated sugar
½ tsp (3g) fine sea salt
1 cup (250ml) whole milk
¾ cup (175ml) heavy whipping cream
6–8 slices bread (such as brioche, **basic sourdough bread, page 54, grocery store white bread, page 64,** or challah)
2 tbsp (28g) **unsalted butter (page 33)**

Options for topping:
Unsalted butter (page 33)
Fresh whipped cream
Fresh fruit
High-quality pure maple syrup
Powdered sugar

1 In a shallow large bowl or a pie dish, whisk together the whole eggs, egg yolks, cinnamon, nutmeg, sugar, and salt until thoroughly combined.

2 Whisk in the milk and heavy cream in a slow, steady stream until you have a homogeneous mixture.

3 Working in batches, add the bread to the liquid and soak on each side for 10 to 25 seconds (less time for very soft bread, and more time for very hard bread).

4 In a 12-inch (30.5-cm) cast-iron skillet, heat the butter over medium heat until hot and bubbling. Swirl the pan to evenly distribute the butter. Working in batches, lay the bread in a single layer in the pan. Toast for 2 to 4 minutes, or until nicely browned and toasted. Flip and toast for an additional 2 to 4 minutes. Repeat this process until you've toasted all of the bread.

5 Enjoy the French toast with the desired toppings: a pat of butter, a dollop of whipped cream, any bite-sized pieces of fruit (if you want to be a little fancy), a generous pour of maple syrup, and a sprinkle of powdered sugar.

ricotta pancakes

There are a bajillion pancake recipes, every one claiming to be the fluffiest. At the end of the day, fluffy pancakes or not, making them yourself instead of from a box is a revolutionary moment. Also, you're saving yourself like maybe 5 minutes by getting a box mix, but losing half of the texture and flavor of homemade. Sounds like a bad deal.

1½ cups (225g) unbleached all-purpose flour
2 tsp (7g) baking powder
¼ tsp (1g) baking soda
2 tbsp (26g) granulated sugar
2 tsp (12g) fine sea salt
Zest of 1 lemon
2 large eggs
1 cup (250ml) whole milk
1 tbsp (15ml) neutral-tasting oil
1 cup (220g) **ricotta (page 38)**
Unsalted butter (page 33) or cooking spray, for greasing

Options for topping:
Salted butter (page 33)
High-quality pure maple syrup
Jam (see **simple jams, page 24**)
Fresh fruit

1 In a medium bowl, whisk together the flour, baking powder, baking soda, sugar, salt, and lemon zest until thoroughly combined.

2 In a separate medium bowl, whisk the eggs. Then whisk in the milk, oil, and ricotta until you have a homogeneous mixture.

3 Add the ricotta-milk mixture to the flour mixture, and whisk until thoroughly combined. It's okay if there are a few lumps. Let the mixture rest for 5 minutes.

4 Heat a large nonstick skillet over medium heat. Lightly grease the pan with butter or spray lightly with cooking spray.

5 Once the pan is hot, add the batter to the pan in ¼-cup measurements, or as desired, spacing them far enough apart to avoid them forming together.

6 Cook the pancakes for 2 to 3 minutes, or until golden brown on the bottom and beginning to bubble on the top. Flip and cook for an additional 2 to 3 minutes, or until just cooked through. Transfer to a plate, and repeat with the rest of the pancake batter. Enjoy with butter, REAL maple syrup, jam, fresh fruit, or whatever you like.

BREAKFAST

PREP TIME:
1 MINUTE + MAKING BREAD, BUTTER, & JAM (IF DESIRED)

COOK TIME:
2–3 MINUTES

YIELD:
1

salted butter & jam toast

Right, so let's talk about the traditions of toast. There are so many throughout history. You've got avocado toast in California, smørrebrød in Scandinavia, pan con tomate in Spain, and this. This right here may be a simple "recipe," but it's something that's very special to me, and I would like you to experience the same thing I do when eating it. And although this is a beautiful way to showcase all your homemade goods, it's not just about the ingredients; it's about the technique.

1 thick slice **grocery store white bread (page 64)** or brioche
1½–3 tbsp (21–42g) **salted butter (page 33)**, softened
2–3 tbsp (40–60g) strawberry or blackberry jam (see **simple jams, page 24**)

1 Toast the bread in a toaster or in the oven just until golden brown. (Do not toast with any cooking fat.)

2 Once the bread is toasted, smear with a very generous amount of butter. There should be a nice visible layer of solid butter on top of the bread.

3 Before the butter melts too much, immediately spread on the jam.

4 Let the toast sit just until the butter melts and soaks into the bread. Enjoy!

austin breakfast tacos

Breakfast tacos and Austin, Texas, are entirely synonymous. I realized that very quickly when I moved there. There are so many variations and arguments about which is the best breakfast taco. Pretty much if you don't start your day at least 2 to 3 times a week with eggs, bacon, and cheese nestled in a lightly charred warm tortilla, then chances are you don't live in Austin. This is an homage to that quintessential breakfast.

8 slices uncooked thick-cut bacon

3 tbsp (42g) **unsalted butter (page 33)**

8–10 large eggs

Kosher salt and freshly cracked black pepper, to taste

8 taco-sized **flour tortillas (page 78)** or corn tortillas

⅓ cup (42g) crumbled cotija cheese

Cilantro leaves, for garnish

Jalapeño salsa (page 45), to serve

1 Line a baking sheet with foil, and arrange the bacon in an even layer on top. Place in a cold oven, and set the oven to 420°F (220°C). Roast the bacon for 20 minutes, or until nicely browned, crispy, and cooked through. Remove the bacon, and let it drain and cool on paper towels.

2 In a large nonstick skillet, heat the butter over medium heat. In a large bowl, whisk the eggs until thoroughly combined. Once the butter is melted and bubbling, add the eggs to the skillet.

3 Constantly stir the eggs, scrambling together the cooked egg with the uncooked egg. Just before the eggs are fully cooked, remove the skillet from the heat. Continue stirring until the eggs are just barely set together and cooked but not rubbery. Season to taste with salt and pepper.

4 If the tortillas aren't already charred from making them first from scratch, heat a medium skillet over medium-high heat. Once hot, working 1 at a time, very lightly char the tortillas on both sides. If the pan is hot enough, this should take 20 to 25 seconds per side. Turn the heat down if they're charring too quickly. If the tortillas are already charred, make sure they're hot and pliable.

5 To assemble the tacos, in the center of each charred tortilla, add a scoop of the scrambled eggs, followed by a strip of cooked bacon, crumbled cotija, cilantro leaves, and jalapeño salsa. Fold as a taco, and serve immediately with more jalapeño salsa to dip.

appetizers... or snacks

I mean, look, at the end of the day sometimes you eat an appetizer as a whole-ass meal, so this can be whatever you want it to be...don't let the world box you in with semantics.

PREP TIME:
25 MINUTES + 1 HOUR 20 MINUTES TO
RISE + MAKING MAYO (IF DESIRED)

COOK TIME:
25 MINUTES

SERVES:
2 DOZEN

pretzel sticks

I don't eat enough pretzels. Not that there is some sort of daily pretzel-eating threshold that must be met...I just know that all of us could probably be a little bit happier if we ate more pretzels. They're satisfying and salty with that classic roasty caramelized dough flavor.

2 cups (500ml) filtered water, heated to about 100°F (38°C)
1/3 cup (72g) firmly packed light brown sugar
3¼ tsp (14g) instant dry yeast
¼ cup (60ml) neutral-tasting oil
5½ cups (825g) unbleached all-purpose flour, plus more for dusting
1 tsp (6g) fine sea salt
Flaky sea salt

Mustard-mayo sauce:
½ cup (115g) **mayonnaise (page 44)**
½ cup (120g) whole-grain mustard
Freshly cracked black pepper, to taste

Lye bath:
1,000g filtered water, room temperature
30g food-grade lye (see note)

1 In a large bowl, mix together the water, brown sugar, and yeast. Cover with plastic wrap and let sit for 10 minutes. The mixture should get lightly foamy, and the yeast should dissolve. Then whisk in the oil.

2 In a separate large bowl, whisk together the flour and fine sea salt. Add the yeast mixture to the flour mixture, and begin mixing by hand until you get a shaggy dough. (The dough may or may not be a little sticky depending on your flour.) Just keep mixing and kneading until the dough starts to pull away from the sides of the bowl.

3 Turn the dough onto a generously floured surface and continue kneading for 3 to 5 minutes, or until smooth and elastic. Transfer the dough to a large greased bowl, cover with greased plastic wrap, and let rise for 45 minutes to 1 hour, or until doubled in size.

4 While the dough is rising, make the mustard-mayo sauce. In a small bowl, mix together all of the ingredients. Cover and refrigerate until ready to use.

5 Preheat the oven to 450°F (230°C). Line 2 or 3 baking sheets with silicone mats. Turn the dough onto an unfloured surface. Punch down the dough to release the gas. Using a kitchen scale for roughly equal pretzels, divide the dough into 24 pieces (60–70g each). Roll each piece into a ball, cover the balls with a damp towel, and allow to rest for 15 minutes. Then roll each ball into an 8-inch (20-cm) stick about ½ inch (1.25cm) thick with slightly tapered ends.

6 Put on rubber or latex food-safe gloves. Be very cautious not to get any of the caustic lye solution on your hands or face. In a large metal or glass bowl, make the lye bath: add the water to the bowl, and whisk in the lye until dissolved.

7 To the lye bath, add 4 to 6 pretzel sticks at a time and soak for 15 to 20 seconds. With gloved hands, carefully transfer the dough to a baking sheet with a 1- to 2-inch (2.5–5-cm) space between each. Leave them in the tube shapes; or for the French epi-shape shown in the photo, cut the pretzels in 3 intervals at a 35-degree angle about three-fourths through the pretzel, and turn each segment in an alternating direction.

8 Sprinkle the pretzels with flaky salt. Bake one sheet at a time for 10 to 15 minutes, or until deep brown. Enjoy while they're still warm with the mustard-mayo sauce for dipping.

note: I know lye seems like a strange addition, but I assure you when done properly, it's perfectly safe to eat. (For one, the concentration of the lye is extraordinarily low, and when baked, it forms a nontoxic carbonate that cements its safety to eat.) A lot of people like to use baking soda, but in my opinion, there is no comparison. A quick dip in a food-grade lye bath is responsible for that deep-brown, blistered crust we all love on a good pretzel.

PREP TIME:
10 MINUTES + MAKING RICOTTA & BREAD (IF DESIRED)

COOK TIME:
1 HOUR

YIELD:
2 CUPS (SERVES 4 AS AN APPETIZER)

whipped ricotta garlic dip

I don't make enough dips in my life. That is, in part, due to the fact that I usually eat way too much of it and afterward feel awful, both physically and emotionally. With that noted, I recommend making sure you have people over when you make this stuff.

2 heads garlic

3 tbsp (45ml) neutral-tasting oil

4 sprigs thyme, plus more thyme leaves for garnish

1 cup (220g) **ricotta (page 38)**

¾ cup (175ml) heavy whipping cream

Zest of 1 lemon, roughly chopped

Flaky sea salt, to taste

$1/3$ cup (42g) finely crushed toasted pistachios

Extra-virgin olive oil, for drizzling

Freshly cracked black pepper, to taste

Crackers, toasted baguette, or toasted **basic sourdough bread (page 54),** to serve

1 Preheat the oven to 325°F (170°C). Cut ¼ to ½ inch (0.5–1.25cm) off the top of the garlic heads to just barely reveal the flesh, keeping the bulbs intact. Discard any loose skin from around the bulbs.

2 Place the bulbs on 2 separate pieces of foil large enough to wrap the bulbs. Drizzle the oil onto the garlic bulbs, coating them evenly. Tightly wrap them in the foil, along with 2 sprigs of thyme in each packet.

3 Place the foil packets on a baking sheet, and cook the garlic for about 1 hour, or until the cloves are very soft and nicely caramelized. Discard the thyme. Let the bulbs sit until cool enough to handle.

4 Squeeze the cloves out of the skins into a small bowl. With a small whisk, beat them until smooth.

5 In a medium bowl, using a handheld mixer, beat the ricotta on high speed until very smooth and lightly aerated. Beat in the heavy cream until thoroughly incorporated. Fold the garlic paste and lemon zest into the whipped ricotta, and season with salt.

6 Transfer the dip to a shallow serving bowl, and top with the pistachios, a generous glug of olive oil, thyme leaves, pepper, and flaky salt. Serve with crackers, toasted baguette slices, or toasted sourdough bread.

cheese board that everyone will eat

Maybe this is too much of a sweeping statement, but I genuinely don't know anyone who doesn't love a good cheese board. (Unless they're lactose intolerant. Although technically most people are, right?) Farting aside, most people will love this cheese board as much as you do.

1 (8 oz/225g) wedge Gruyère cheese, cold
1 (8 oz/225g) wheel triple creme Brie cheese, cold
1 (8 oz/225g) batch **chèvre (page 38),** cold
2–3 pickle varieties of choice (see **pickled anything, page 20**), such as red onions and cornichons
½ cup (160g) strawberry or blackberry jam (see **simple jams, page 24**)
¼ cup (60g) whole-grain mustard
Fresh fruit (such as red and green grapes, pears, kumquats, and strawberries), sliced as desired
Toasted slices of bread (such as **basic sourdough bread, page 54** or **big boy miche, page 57**)

1 Arrange all of the components on a large platter, using ramekins to hold the chèvre, jam, mustard, and any loose pickles. (Okay, I admit this is more of a suggestion rather than an actual recipe.)

2 Place small teaspoons and cheese knives for serving. Enjoy immediately.

APPETIZERS...OR SNACKS

PREP TIME:
5 MINUTES + MAKING MAYO (IF DESIRED)

COOK TIME:
45 MINUTES

SERVES:
4

smashed patatas bravas

Everyone has that friend who tells way too many stories about "being in Europe" to the point they're borderline talking down to you...okay, well let me be that friend for a second. The first time I went to Spain, I went to a multitude of tapas bars, most of which had this item I kept seeing over and over: patatas bravas. It sounded super fancy, but I was actually underwhelmed to see what it was—in essence, just a potato dish with a spicy tomato sauce and usually a garlic mayo. Yeah, well I took my first bite, and immediately it was one of my most enjoyed pieces of food while I was there.

1 lb (450g) baby
  potatoes
2½ tbsp (40ml) extra-
  virgin olive oil
Kosher salt, to taste
Mayonnaise (page 44),
  to serve (see note)
Cilantro leaves (optional),
  for garnish

Bravas sauce:
3 tbsp (45ml) extra-virgin
  olive oil
1 medium sweet onion,
  diced
Kosher salt, to taste
1 tbsp (7g) smoked
  paprika
2 tsp (5g) sweet paprika
4 cloves garlic, roughly
  chopped
1 (14 oz/400g) can
  crushed tomatoes
  (undrained)
1½ tsp (7g) granulated
  sugar

1 Boil the potatoes until soft and easily pierced with a fork. Drain and let dry until the skins are no longer wet. About 10 minutes into the cooking time, preheat the oven to 425°F (220°C).

2 While the potatoes are cooking, make the bravas sauce. In a medium saucepan, heat the olive oil over medium heat until shimmering and hot. Add the onions, and season with salt, smoked paprika, and sweet paprika. Cook, stirring occasionally, until the onion begins to soften. Then add the garlic and cook until fragrant.

3 Stir in the crushed tomatoes and sugar. Simmer, stirring occasionally, for about 15 minutes, or until the sauce is reduced by about 25 percent. Taste and season with salt. If desired, blend the sauce to a smooth consistency, or serve it as is.

4 Place the cooked and dried potatoes in a roasting tray or on a foil-lined baking sheet. Using the bottom of a flat cup, slightly flatten the potatoes until craggy on the sides but still holding their shape.

5 Drizzle the potatoes with the olive oil and season to taste with salt. Cook for about 25 minutes, or until deep golden in color and crispy on the outside.

6 Serve the potatoes with the bravas sauce and mayonnaise. (I like to pour the mayo and bravas sauce into squirt bottles and add little alternating dots of each all over the potatoes for a fun presentation.) Garnish with cilantro leaves (if using), and enjoy.

note: The mayonnaise to me is not optional because it provides richness and texture in the dish. I like adding a little bit of grated garlic—1 or 2 cloves per 1 cup of mayonnaise—just to give it a garlicky kick in the pants.

PREP TIME:
**5 MINUTES + MAKING
BREAD, BUTTER, & EGGS
(IF DESIRED)**

COOK TIME:
2 MINUTES

SERVES:
4

avocado & egg toast

Alright, I might be from LA, and I also might have an avocado toast recipe in this book—truly the ultimate stereotype. But let's all just take a real step back and look at avocado toast. It is f—ing delicious. I don't care who you are. If you enjoy avocado, it's one of the greatest little snacks (or even a whole meal) that I can think to have. It's perfectly rich and exciting to eat, yet you don't feel sloppy after eating it. It's a win-win.

4 slices **basic
  sourdough bread
  (page 54)**
**Unsalted butter
  (page 33;** optional),
  for toasting
1 clove garlic
1 very ripe tomato
1 large avocado
Sichuan chili oil or spicy
  chili crisp, for drizzling
4 **perfect soft-boiled
  eggs (page 90),**
  warm, quartered
Flaky sea salt, for garnish
Torn Thai basil or regular
  basil, for garnish

1 Toast the bread either in a pan with butter or in a toaster.

2 Cut the garlic clove in half, and rub the cut sides all over each slice of toast to perfume with garlic. Cut the tomato in half and repeat the same technique with the cut sides of the tomato. (Get the juice all up in there; that's what you want.)

3 Slice the avocado thinly and arrange in a shingled pattern on the toast. Drizzle with the chili oil, top each slice with a soft-boiled egg, and finish with a generous pinch of salt and some torn basil.

fish

If you don't like fish, then this is not the place for you.
Just kidding. This is the place for you to start enjoying fish.

PREP TIME:
**20 MINUTES + MAKING
SAUCE GRIBICHE**

COOK TIME:
20 MINUTES

SERVES:
4–5

beer-battered fish

This is essentially the fish to your chips. I'm not including the chips for one main reason: I think it's important to really focus on frying fish perfectly. French fries can be really easy, but fish, on the other hand, is usually quite challenging. To that I say, "No. No more." You don't need it to be fancy—you only need to focus on technique.

2 lb (1kg) cod, cut into
   5 x 2-inch (12.5 x 5-cm)
   pieces
High-heat oil (such as
   canola, avocado,
   vegetable, lard, etc.),
   for frying
1½ cups (225g)
   unbleached all-
   purpose flour, divided
1 tbsp (7g) paprika
1 tbsp (10g) garlic
   powder
2 tsp (5g) white pepper
2½ tsp (15g) fine sea salt,
   plus more to season
1 large egg
12 oz (340g) light beer
   (such as lager)
**Sauce gribiche
   (page 48),** to serve

1 Season the cod generously with salt on all sides. Place on paper towels and let sit at room temperature for 15 minutes. A good amount of water will drain from the fish—that's what you want.

2 Fill a large, deep cast-iron skillet or heavy-bottomed pot just over halfway, or about 2 inches (5cm), with the oil. Fit with a fry thermometer or candy thermometer, and heat the oil to 365°F (185°C). Adjust the heat up and down to maintain that temperature.

3 In a small bowl, add ½ cup (60g) flour. In a medium bowl, whisk together the remaining 1 cup (120g) flour, paprika, garlic powder, white pepper, and salt until thoroughly combined. Whisk in the egg; it will get clumpy and shaggy. Slowly begin whisking in the beer until all of it is added. Once you have a smooth batter (try to avoid beating it to a frothy mess), it's ready.

4 Gently toss the fish pieces in the dry flour from the small bowl to coat thoroughly, and shake off the excess. Then dip the fish pieces into the batter. Working in batches so you don't overcrowd the skillet, carefully drop the fish pieces into the oil and fry for 3 to 5 minutes, flipping once halfway through, until golden brown and crispy. Using a kitchen spider or pair of tongs, gently remove the fried fish and place on a wire rack to drain. Repeat in batches with the remaining fish.

5 Serve immediately with the sauce gribiche.

PREP TIME:
15 MINUTES + MAKING FISH, MAYO, PICKLES, & HOT SAUCE (IF DESIRED)

COOK TIME:
5 MINUTES

SERVES:
4 (2 TACOS PER PERSON)

fried fish tacos

In general, I think just the idea of a "fish taco" gets a bad rap. Maybe it's because people are too busy thinking about something more familiar, like a carnitas or steak taco. I'm here to tell you that if there is anything to convert you to the world of fish tacos, this is it right here.

16 taco-sized corn tortillas
1 batch **beer-battered fish (page 128;** exclude the sauce gribiche)
Cilantro leaves (optional), for garnish
Pickled jalapeños (see **pickled anything, page 20;** optional), for garnish
Lime slices (optional), to serve

Crema:
½ cup (123g) sour cream
½ cup (115g) **mayonnaise (page 44)**
1 tbsp (15ml) **hot sauce (page 41)**
2 tsp (5g) smoked paprika
1 tbsp (15ml) chili oil
1½ tbsp (20ml) Chinese black rice vinegar
2 cloves garlic, grated
Kosher salt, to taste

Slaw:
½ head green cabbage, very thinly sliced
½ large red onion, thinly sliced
2 medium carrots, julienned
½ cup (8g) finely chopped cilantro
Zest and juice of 2 meyer or regular lemons
2 tbsp (30ml) extra-virgin olive oil
Kosher salt and freshly cracked black pepper, to taste

1 Make the crema. In a small bowl, whisk together the sour cream, mayonnaise, hot sauce, smoked paprika, chili oil, vinegar, and garlic. Season to taste generously with salt. Set aside until ready to serve.

2 Make the slaw. In a medium bowl, toss together the cabbage, onion, carrots, and cilantro until incorporated. Add the zest and juice of the lemons and the olive oil, and season to taste with salt and pepper. Toss again to thoroughly distribute, and set aside for at least 5 minutes or until ready to serve.

3 Heat a medium skillet over medium-high heat. Once hot, working 1 at a time, very lightly char the tortillas on both sides. If the pan is hot enough, this should take 20 to 25 seconds per side. Turn the heat down if they're charring too quickly.

4 Assemble each taco by stacking 2 tortillas per taco. Top with the beer-battered fish, the slaw, and a generous drizzle of the crema. Garnish with cilantro leaves and pickled jalapeños (if using). Add a squeeze of lime juice (if using). Fold as a taco, and enjoy!

PREP TIME:
**25 MINUTES + MAKING PICKLES
(IF DESIRED)**

COOK TIME:
15 MINUTES

SERVES:
4

grilled branzino

I learned this genius grilling technique for fillets of fish when I worked at Uchiko. Rather than setting the fish directly on the grates and going into a deep panic when it sticks, you instead use a greased wire rack to easily maneuver the fish around the heat source. This helps the fish maintain contact with the heat until it's browned enough to release. Don't tell anyone I told you this secret. Also, yes, you should be eating the skin.

¼ cup (4g) cilantro leaves
¼ cup (5g) Thai basil leaves
¼ cup (8g) mint leaves
¼ cup (26g) thinly sliced green onions
¼ cup (55g) pickled red onions (see **pickled anything, page 20**)
Flaky sea salt, to serve
Chili oil, to drizzle
Lime wedges (optional), to serve

Coconut broth:
1 (14 fl oz/400ml) can unsweetened full-fat coconut milk
2 stalks lemongrass, bruised and thinly sliced
1 shallot, thinly sliced
2-inch (5-cm) piece fresh galangal or ginger, peeled and thinly sliced
1 tbsp (15ml) fish sauce
1 tbsp (13g) palm sugar or light brown sugar
Juice of 1 lime
Kosher salt, to taste

Fish:
4 fillets branzino (about 1½ lb/680g total), scaled and skin-on
Cooking spray, to coat
Kosher salt, to taste

1 Make the coconut broth. In a medium saucepan, combine the coconut milk, lemongrass, shallot, and galangal. Heat over medium heat just until steamy and hot. Turn off the heat, and cover to steep for 12 minutes. Strain the broth through a fine-mesh strainer into a small bowl, and discard the solids. Whisk in the fish sauce, palm sugar, and lime juice. Season with salt to taste. Keep the broth hot in the saucepan.

2 In a small bowl, toss together the cilantro, Thai basil, mint, green onion, and pickled red onions. Cover with a lightly damp paper towel, and refrigerate until ready to use.

3 Heat 1 side of the grill to medium-high, and keep the other side completely off. Let the grill preheat with the lid closed for 10 minutes.

4 Generously spray a grill-safe, 8 x 10-inch (20 x 25-cm) wire rack with cooking spray. Prepare the fish. Pat the fillets dry with paper towels, and spray the skin lightly with cooking spray. Season both sides of each fillet with salt to taste. Place the fillets skin-side down on the wire rack. (You can usually fit 1 or 2 fillets on 1 wire rack, so cook them in batches or with 1 additional wire rack as needed.)

5 Once the grill is hot, place the wire rack with the fish directly over the hot side of the grill. Let the fish grill for about 3 minutes, checking the skin intermittently, until the skin is completely crisp and lightly charred and you can see the fish is cooked about halfway up the flesh. Using a thin spatula, carefully flip the fish. Cook skin-side up, until the fish is JUST barely cooked through, another 30 to 60 seconds. In the event the fish is cooking too quickly, shift the rack toward the cold side of the grill. Once cooked, remove from the grill and let rest on a cutting board, uncovered and skin-side up, while you cook any remaining batches.

6 For serving, add about ½ inch (1.25cm) of hot broth to 4 small, deep plates or very shallow serving bowls. Gently lay the fish flesh-side down into the broth. Top the fish with the herb mixture and flaky salt. Finish with a drizzle of chili oil. Enjoy with lime wedges on the side (if using).

PREP TIME:
15 MINUTES + 20 MINUTES OR OVERNIGHT TO BRINE

COOK TIME:
6 MINUTES

SERVES:
4

the easiest crispy skin fish

A lot of people are picky about fish. In my opinion, too many. My firm belief is that of those people, the majority of them just haven't had a beautifully cooked piece of fish. If executed properly, this recipe should be able to change that.

4 fillets skin-on red snapper, grouper, or other white fish (about 1½ lb/680g total)

Kosher salt, to taste

2½ tbsp (40ml) neutral-tasting oil

3 tbsp (45ml) extra-virgin olive oil

2 tbsp (6g) thinly sliced chives

Flaky sea salt, to garnish

1 Season the fillets generously with salt. Let rest at room temperature for 20 minutes, or overnight, covered, in the refrigerator. This firms the flesh, and the salt seasons the center of the fish.

2 In a 12-inch (30.5-cm) skillet, heat the neutral-tasting oil over medium-high heat for 2 to 3 minutes, or until very hot.

3 Pat the fillets dry and place skin-side down in the skillet. Because the skin can curl dramatically at first, hold the fish down with a spatula or spoon until it lays flat.

4 Sear the fish until you can see the flesh cooked about halfway up and the skin is crispy, 2 to 3 minutes. Flip, being careful not to rip the skin. Sear for another 2 to 3 minutes, or until the two cooked sides of flesh just barely meet each other. Immediately remove the cooked fillets from the pan.

5 In a small bowl, mix the olive oil and chives until combined. Serve the fish dressed generously with the chive dressing, and garnish with flaky salt.

PREP TIME:
**20 MINUTES + MAKING
MAYO (IF DESIRED)**

COOK TIME:
10–15 MINUTES

SERVES:
4

parmesan & nut crusted salmon

I'll be honest: crusted salmon is overrated to me. Big time. And yet I can't stop myself when I'm around this one. It's my culinary kryptonite. That and a big bowl of queso, but not necessarily in the same meal.

4 skin-on salmon fillets (about 2 lb/1kg total)
¼ cup (58g) **mayonnaise (page 44)**
2½ tbsp (38g) whole-grain mustard
3 cloves garlic, freshly grated
Kosher salt, to taste
Freshly grated black truffle (optional)
½ cup (45g) toasted walnut halves
½ cup (45g) toasted pecan halves
½ cup (40g) freshly grated Parmigiano-Reggiano cheese
1–2 tbsp (4–8g) chopped flat-leaf parsley
Freshly cracked black pepper, to taste
Lemon wedges or champagne vinegar (optional), to serve

1 Preheat the oven to 425°F (220°C). Line a rimmed baking sheet with parchment paper, and evenly arrange the fillets on top.

2 In a small bowl, stir together the mayonnaise, mustard, garlic, and salt to taste. Mix until thoroughly combined. Grate in a few tablespoons black truffle (if using), and mix together.

3 In a resealable plastic bag, add the walnuts and pecans. Crush into fine- to medium-sized pieces. (I bang on them with a heavy pot.) Pour into a large bowl, and add the Parmigiano-Reggiano, parsley, and salt and pepper to taste. Mix together until thoroughly combined.

4 Season each fillet on all sides with salt, and brush generously with the mayonnaise mixture. Top with a generous amount of the cheesy-nut mixture.

5 Roast for 10 to 15 minutes, or to your liking. Plate and enjoy with lemon wedges or champagne vinegar (if desired) to cut the richness.

FISH

PREP TIME:
**20 MINUTES + STEAMING LOBSTER +
MAKING MAYO, BUTTER, & BUNS (IF DESIRED)**

COOK TIME:
5 MINUTES

SERVES:
4

maine-style lobster rolls

Originally, I was not going to include a lobster roll recipe. I know all the lobster roll regions of America are going to have something to say about it. (Can you guys just stay calm and stuff that yapper of yours with a big meaty claw or something?) But we have this beautiful multipurpose dough that makes the most gorgeous hot dog buns—or in this case lobster roll buns—so it claimed its seat at our table.

2 large lobsters,
  steamed (see note)
  and chilled
1/3 cup (77g)
  **mayonnaise
  (page 44)**
Zest and juice of
  1 lemon, plus more
  zest to garnish
1 tbsp (4g) finely sliced
  chives, plus more
  to garnish
1 tbsp (3g) finely
  chopped dill
2 tsp (2g) finely chopped
  tarragon
Kosher salt and freshly
  cracked black pepper,
  to taste
4 hot dog buns
  (see **my famous
  multipurpose dough,
  pages 60–63;** the sides
  of the buns should be
  flat if you follow the
  way I make them)
4 tbsp (56g) **unsalted
  butter (page 33),**
  softened

1 Crack the lobster shells and remove the meat (in one piece, as possible). Set on a paper towel to drain slightly.

2 In a medium bowl, add the mayonnaise, lemon zest and juice, chives, dill, tarragon, and salt and pepper to taste. Whisk together until thoroughly combined. Leave the lobster whole, if desired, or cut it into large bite-sized pieces. Once you've finally made that decision, add the lobster to the mayonnaise mixture, and toss to coat evenly.

3 With a sharp knife, split the buns and carefully open them. Spread the softened butter on the inside of the buns. Place them butter-side down in a cold nonstick pan, and place over medium heat. Toast for 2 minutes, or until golden brown.

4 Stuff the buns with the lobster salad. Top with additional sliced chives, pepper, and lemon zest, and enjoy!

note: So, please do me a favor—dispatch your lobsters humanely if you choose to go the live lobster route. Boiling them alive isn't the greatest choice. Instead, I recommend kindly letting them leave this world (with the help of a knife) prior to steaming or boiling them. Find a video of how to do this correctly online. I would describe it here, but I genuinely think it needs visual instruction to do it properly.

gravlax smørrebrød

If you know me, then you know I'm not always great at pronouncing things. Good luck trying to pronounce this one properly. Thankfully, you don't need to be able to say it (*grahv-locks smuhr-brot*), or know that it means "salmon in a grave butter and bread," in order to make it. This Danish classic is a simple open-faced sandwich with salmon, and although there are traditions involved here, there's a little bit of wiggle room, too. Kate, if you're reading, this one is for you and the Danish in you and your family! Love you!

4 (1-inch-/2.5-cm- thick) slices crusty **basic sourdough bread (page 54)**
Unsalted butter (page 33; optional), to toast
1 shallot, very thinly sliced into rings
8–12 slices gravlax or smoked salmon
2 radishes, very thinly sliced
Dill, for garnish
Caviar (optional—if you wanna be bougie), for garnish

Horseradish-chive cream:
½ cup (120g) crème fraîche
Zest and juice of 1 lemon
2 tsp (4g) freshly grated horseradish
1 clove garlic, grated
½ bunch of chives, thinly sliced
2 tsp (2g) finely chopped dill
Kosher salt and freshly cracked black pepper, to taste

1 Make the horseradish-chive cream. In a medium bowl, whisk together the crème fraîche, zest and juice of the lemon, horseradish, garlic, chives, and dill until thoroughly combined. Season to taste with salt and pepper. (Make sure not to undersalt this; it needs a little more than you think.) Set aside.

2 Toast the bread however you would like. (I usually toast mine in a pan with butter, but a regular toaster oven, and without butter, works great, too.) Let the toast cool slightly so it's not ripping hot.

3 While the toast is cooling, in a small bowl, cover the shallots with water. Drain and repeat two more times (to help reduce the aggressive bite of the shallots). Drain well.

4 Spread a generous amount of the horseradish-chive cream onto the slices of toast. Top with 2 to 3 gravlax slices. Garnish with the radish slices, the rinsed shallot rings, and finally the fresh dill. Really take your time here—make it look beautiful. Top with caviar (if using) because it's a classic flavor on this and also for the flex. (Or don't. It's not necessary at all.) Enjoy!

meat

Yes, we have THE MEAT.

PREP TIME:
**8 MINUTES + MAKING
BUTTER (IF DESIRED)**

COOK TIME:
8 MINUTES

SERVES:
2

the perfect steak

This recipe can sometimes cause a little controversy unless you already KNOW about its power. You can tell it's powerful just by looking at it. This method is an old-school steakhouse secret that every human being on the planet should know.

2 ribeye or New York
    strip steaks (1¼–
    1½ inches/3–3.75cm
    thick)
Kosher salt and freshly
    cracked black pepper,
    to taste
2½ tbsp (40ml) neutral-
    tasting oil
4 tbsp (56g) **unsalted
    butter (page 33)**
1 bunch of thyme
3 cloves garlic, skin-on
    and lightly crushed

1 Pat the steaks completely dry on all sides. Season the steaks very generously with salt and pepper. (Go a little heavier than normal; don't be shy.)

2 Preheat a medium skillet over medium-high heat. Add the oil, and heat until extremely hot and nearly smoking.

3 Carefully place 1 or 2 steaks in the pan, depending on their size; you want at least 1 inch (2.5cm) of separation, so cook in batches as necessary. Sear for 2 to 3 minutes, or until you get a deep brown crust on the bottom from edge to edge. Flip and sear for an additional 2 to 3 minutes. (If the steaks are the specified thickness, they should be very close to reaching medium rare at this point; if thicker, cook slightly longer.)

4 With the heat still on, add the butter, bunch of thyme, and garlic in the skins. Baste the steaks repeatedly until they reach medium-rare, an internal temperature of 132°F (56°C). (They will coast the rest of the way to 135°F/57°C, which is technically medium-rare.)

5 Remove the steaks from the pan and let rest, uncovered, for 5 minutes before slicing. Enjoy!

MEAT

144

PREP TIME:
20 MINUTES + OVERNIGHT TO MARINATE +
MAKING STOCK (IF NEEDED)

COOK TIME:
3½ HOURS

YIELD:
2½ QT (2½ LITERS)

mojo-braised pulled pork

This succulent, flavorful meat is endlessly versatile. It goes well with beans, rice, and vegetables for a classic Cuban-style dinner, or in tacos, on Cubanos (page 178), or just by itself.

4–5 lb (2–2.25kg)
  boneless pork
  shoulder or
  Boston butt
Chicken stock (see
  **basic stock out of
  anything, page 28**),
  if needed
Kosher salt, to taste

Mojo marinade:
2 shallots
2 heads garlic, peeled
Zest of 2 oranges
Zest of 3 limes
2 tbsp (7g) oregano
  leaves
½ bunch of mint leaves
1 tbsp (5g) freshly
  ground cumin
2 serrano chilies
1 cup (250ml) extra-
  virgin olive oil
1½ tbsp (27g) kosher
  salt
1 cup (250ml) fresh lime
  juice or Seville orange
  juice
1 cup (250ml) fresh
  orange juice

1 Prepare the mojo marinade. In a blender, add the shallots, garlic cloves, orange zest, lime zest, oregano leaves, mint leaves, freshly ground cumin, serrano chilies, olive oil, salt, lime juice, and orange juice. Blend together on high speed until completely smooth. Reserve 1 cup (250ml) of the marinade to use for dipping; refrigerate, covered, until needed.

2 In a large resealable bag, place the pork shoulder, and pour in the remaining mojo marinade to cover the meat. Seal the bag and marinate in the refrigerator overnight.

3 Preheat the oven to 400°F (200°C). Remove the pork from the marinade and place in a 7-quart (6.5-liter) Dutch oven. Pour in all of the marinade. The marinade should come about halfway up the pot, but if not, add a little bit of chicken stock.

4 Braise the pork, uncovered, for 10 minutes. Then reduce the temperature to 350°F (180°C) and cook for 3 to 3½ hours, uncovered, turning occasionally to make sure all sides get browned.

5 Remove the pork from the Dutch oven and place on a cutting board to cool.

6 Strain the remaining mojo braising liquid into a small bowl, discarding the solids.

7 In a large bowl, using two forks, shred the meat. Toss together using the strained braising liquid to coat the meat to your desired level of fatty goodness. Season to taste with salt. Enjoy in Cubanos (page 178), on rice, or in a quesadilla with the reserved marinade for dipping.

MEAT

chicken parmesan

The Italian bistro classic, the New York City street corner bite at 10 p.m. after having one too many Aperol spritzes—there are very few things as beautiful as a stunning chicken Parmesan. This recipe will bring happiness to everyone who eats it.

4 boneless, skinless chicken breasts (about 1½ lb/680g total)
Kosher salt, to taste
High-heat oil (such as canola, avocado, vegetable, lard, etc.), for frying
270g fresh **mozzarella (page 36;** about 3½ cups), grated
70g fresh Parmigiano-Reggiano cheese (about ¾ cup), grated
Thinly sliced chives (optional), for serving

Breading:
1½ cups (225g) unbleached all-purpose flour
1 tbsp (18g) fine sea salt
Freshly cracked black pepper, to taste
4 large eggs plus a splash of filtered water
2½ cups (275g) plain panko

Sauce:
3–4 slices uncooked thick-cut bacon or pancetta
2½ tbsp (40ml) extra-virgin olive oil
2 red Fresno or Thai chilies, finely diced
1 tsp (2g) red pepper flakes
5 cloves garlic, thinly sliced
1 (28 oz/800g) can crushed San Marzano tomatoes
Kosher salt and freshly cracked black pepper, to taste
Pinch of granulated sugar
5 sprigs thyme (optional), tied together with kitchen twine
¼ cup (62g) freshly grated Parmigiano-Reggiano cheese

1 Prepare the sauce. Slice the bacon or pancetta into ½ inch (1.25cm) pieces and place in a cold medium saucepan. Place over medium heat, and add the olive oil. Stir often. Once the bacon starts to become crispy, add the chilies, red pepper flakes, and garlic. Continue cooking over medium heat until fragrant and the aromatics are toasted.

2 Remove all of the solids to a cutting board, leaving the oil in the pan over the heat. Reduce the heat to low. Very finely chop the bacon mixture and then place back into the pan.

3 Increase the heat to medium, and add the crushed tomatoes. Season to taste with kosher salt and pepper, and stir in a pinch of sugar. Add the thyme bundle (if using) and the Parmigiano-Reggiano, stirring to fully combine. Let the sauce simmer for 15 minutes, stirring occasionally. Pour into a bowl, remove the thyme bundle (if used), and set aside.

4 While the sauce is simmering, prepare the chicken. Carefully butterfly the chicken breasts, but not all the way through, leaving one edge intact like a hinge. Place a piece of plastic wrap over the opened chicken pieces, and pound the chicken breasts until they are slightly thinner than ½ inch (1.25cm) thick. Season lightly with kosher salt.

5 Fill a large deep cast-iron skillet or heavy-bottomed pot just over halfway, or about 2 inches (5cm), with oil. Fit with a fry thermometer or candy thermometer, and heat the oil to 350°F (180°C). Adjust the heat up and down to maintain that temperature.

6 While the oil is heating, prepare 3 separate shallow bowls for the breading station. In the first, whisk together the all-purpose flour, fine sea salt, and pepper to taste. In the second, beat the eggs with a splash of water. In the third, place the panko.

7 Coat each piece of chicken in the all-purpose flour, shaking off the excess. Then dip into the egg wash to thoroughly coat so no dry spots remain. Finally, coat in the panko, pressing the chicken into the crumbs to thoroughly coat. Place to the side, and repeat with the remaining chicken breasts.

8 Cooking 1 at a time, carefully place the breaded chicken breast into the oil (dropping away from you). Fry on one side for 3 to 5 minutes, or until crispy golden brown and then flip and fry for an additional 3 to 5 minutes, or until it reaches an internal temperature of 165°F (75°C). Place on a wire rack in a rimmed baking sheet to cool. Repeat with the remaining chicken.

9 After all of the chicken is fried, in a large bowl, toss together the grated mozzarella and Parmigiano-Reggiano.

10 Preheat the broiler. Place the crispy chicken pieces on 2 foil-lined baking sheets. Cover each piece generously with the sauce, and generously top with the cheese mixture.

11 Working 1 baking sheet at a time, place under the broiler for 5 to 8 minutes, or until the cheese is completely melted and golden brown. Plate, garnish with thinly sliced chives (if using), and enjoy.

PREP TIME:
35 MINUTES + MAKING KATSU SAUCE (IF DESIRED)

COOK TIME:
40 MINUTES

SERVES:
4

chicken katsu

Ol' reliable when I go out to eat at a Japanese restaurant is a nice plate of chicken katsu, some rice, and maybe some vegetables. It's a beauty-in-simplicity moment—ultra-crispy Japanese fried chicken smothered in a sweet and tangy sauce. The world fell in love with it long ago, and for good reason.

4 boneless, skinless chicken breasts or thighs (about 1½ lb/680g total)
Kosher salt, to season
1½ cups (225g) unbleached all-purpose flour
3 large eggs
2 tbsp (30ml) filtered water
2 cups (210g) plain panko
2 cups (500ml) high-heat oil (such as canola, avocado, vegetable, lard, etc.), for frying
Katsu sauce (page 49), to serve

Cabbage slaw:
½ head green cabbage, thinly sliced
Kosher salt, to taste
½ bunch of green onions, thinly sliced
Spicy chili garlic topping or chili oil, to taste
Fresh lemon juice, to taste

1 Place the chicken breasts between 2 pieces of plastic wrap and pound to an even thickness throughout, about ½ inch (1.25cm) thick. Season the chicken with salt.

2 Prepare 3 separate shallow bowls for the breading station. In the first, place the all-purpose flour. In the second, whisk together the eggs and water. In the last, place the panko.

3 Thoroughly coat each piece of chicken in the flour, shaking off any excess. Then coat evenly in the egg mixture, making sure no dry spots remain. Finally, coat the chicken on all sides in the panko, pressing to make sure it's thoroughly coated. Set aside on a piece of parchment paper, and separate each breast with a new layer of parchment.

4 Fill a large deep cast-iron skillet or heavy-bottomed pot with the oil, and heat over medium-high heat until just shimmering, or about 325 to 350°F (170–180°C).

5 Working 1 at a time, carefully place the breaded chicken breast in the oil (dropping away from you). Fry for 3 to 5 minutes, or until crispy golden brown. Flip and fry for an additional 3 to 5 minutes, or until it reaches an internal temperature of 165°F (75°C). Place on a wire rack in a rimmed baking sheet, season again with salt, and let drain and cool. Repeat with the remaining chicken breasts.

6 Make the spicy cabbage slaw. In a medium bowl, toss the cabbage with some kosher salt, and bruise it by squeezing a few times. Add the green onions, chili garlic or oil, and lemon juice. Toss to combine. Taste and adjust the flavors as desired. Plate the katsu and enjoy with the katsu sauce and slaw, or assemble into a sandwich on white bread.

note: Pound and season the raw chicken up to 1 day in advance, refrigerating it overnight so it's extra flavorful. You can also refrigerate the breaded, uncooked chicken overnight.

PREP TIME:
5 MINUTES + MAKING BUTTER (IF DESIRED)

COOK TIME:
10 MINUTES

SERVES:
4

perfect pork chops

Pork chops are very important to me, and they should be important to you, too. They usually get the short end of the stick in terms of cookery, but if you treat a beautiful pork chop like a fine and expensive steak, there is a juicy world of reward awaiting you on the other side.

4 (1-inch/2.5-cm thick) bone-in pork loin chops

Kosher salt and freshly cracked black pepper, to taste

Seasonings of choice (optional), such as curry powder or other spice blend

3 tbsp (45ml) neutral-tasting oil

4 tbsp (56g) **unsalted butter (page 33)**

1 bunch of sage

5 cloves garlic, smashed

Juice of ½ lemon

1 Season all sides of the pork chops generously with salt and pepper. Sprinkle with more seasonings (if using).

2 In a large skillet, heat the oil over medium-high heat. Once the pan is ripping hot, add the pork chops, working in batches if needed so there is no overcrowding. Sear for 3 minutes, or until beautifully browned. Flip and reduce the heat to medium. Cook for another 3 to 5 minutes, or until the internal temperature is 135°F (57°C).

3 Add the butter, sage, and garlic to the pan. Leaving the heat on medium, continuously baste the pork chops by spooning the melted butter over the chops until they reach an internal temperature of 145°F (65°C).

4 Squeeze the lemon over the pork chops. Remove them to a plate and let rest, uncovered, for 5 minutes. Enjoy!

155

chicken breasts that are actually good

I don't want to hear anyone complaining to me about the equipment I use in this recipe. If you want to reach an absolutely perfectly cooked chicken breast with little to no effort, a sous vide is the easiest way to do it. If you want another cooking method, go to my YouTube channel or search a different one, but this recipe is nearly foolproof.

2–4 boneless, skinless chicken breasts (¾–1½ lb/340–680g total)
Kosher salt and freshly cracked black pepper, to taste
Seasonings and aromatics of choice, such as smoked paprika, vadouvan curry powder, or za'atar
2 tbsp (30ml) neutral-tasting oil

1 Set up a sous vide circulator in a 7-quart (6.5-liter) container filled about three-fourths full of water. Preheat to 156°F (69°C).

2 Season the chicken breasts generously with salt and pepper to taste and any other seasonings you desire. Place in 1 or 2 vacuum bags. Add the aromatics of choice to the bags, and vacuum seal.

3 Once the water is to temperature, add the bag of chicken and cook for at least 1 hour and up to 1½ hours; don't worry about them overcooking.

4 Once cooked, you can either chill the chicken in the bag in an ice water bath and then refrigerate for up to 3 days to use in whatever you want or remove the chicken from the bag, pat dry, and use immediately. Discard the herbs.

5 Before serving the chicken, in a large skillet, heat the oil over medium-high heat. Once the pan is very hot, add the chicken breasts and sear for 2 minutes, or until nicely browned on the bottom. Flip and sear on the other side until nicely browned. You just want color here, so try not to cook it much more while doing this.

6 Remove the chicken from the pan and let rest, uncovered, for 3 to 4 minutes before slicing. Enjoy with whatever you like!

MEAT

restaurant-style duck breasts

If you've ever been served the duck breast at an upscale restaurant and it made you "ooh" and "ahhh," then that duck was expertly prepared. It's arguably one of the easiest items for a line cook, yet the result is a jaw-dropping succulent duck.

2–4 skin-on duck
   breasts (1¾–3½ lb/
   790g–1.6kg)
Kosher salt and freshly
   cracked black pepper,
   to taste

1 Using a sharp knife, lightly score the duck skin in a crosshatch pattern; make sure not to penetrate all the way to the meat. Season each duck breast generously with salt on both sides.

2 Place the duck breasts skin-side down in a large cold pan, making sure there is at least 1 inch (2.5cm) of space between each. Cook over medium heat, undisturbed, until the fat renders out and the skin is a gorgeous golden-brown color and crispy, about 5 minutes.

3 Flip the duck breasts and increase the heat to medium-high. Sear on the other side for 2 to 3 minutes, or until the internal temperature reaches 137°F (58°C) for medium-rare.

4 Remove the breasts from the pan and let rest for 3 to 5 minutes. Thinly slice and season with freshly cracked black pepper. Enjoy with whatever you like! (And definitely save that rendered duck fat for another use!)

MEAT

PREP TIME:
45 MINUTES + 20 MINUTES OR OVERNIGHT TO MARINATE + MAKING BUTTER (IF DESIRED)

COOK TIME:
25–40 MINUTES

SERVES:
4

mom's chicken fried steak

The cliche "Oh, when I was a child…" moment is about to happen. But really, the most nostalgic foods of my life are the soul foods my mom has always cooked for me. At the top of that list is her incredibly crispy and tender chicken fried steak, smothered in an unctuous, rich, creamy gravy. It hits the spot so you can hit the pillow when you're done eating it.

4 tenderized cube steaks (1–1½ lb/450–680g total; ask your butcher to flatten and tenderize them for you)

Whole milk or buttermilk, to cover

2 sleeves (258g) saltine crackers, coarsely crushed

1½ cups (225g) unbleached all-purpose flour

2½ tbsp (45g) kosher salt

Freshly cracked black pepper, to taste

High-heat oil (such as canola, avocado, vegetable, lard, etc.), for frying

Cream gravy:
½ cup (125ml) neutral-tasting oil or **unsalted butter (page 33)**

²/₃ cup (100g) unbleached all-purpose flour

2 cups (500ml) whole milk, plus more if needed

Kosher salt and freshly cracked black pepper, to taste

1 Place the cube steaks in an 8-inch (20-cm) square baking dish, and pour in whole milk to cover. Marinate at room temperature for 15 to 20 minutes or covered overnight in the refrigerator.

2 Place the coarsely crushed crackers in a large deep baking dish, along with the all-purpose flour, salt, and pepper to taste. Mix together until thoroughly combined.

3 Fill a large deep cast-iron skillet or heavy-bottomed pot with about 1 inch (2.5cm) of the oil. Heat over medium-high heat until it begins to shimmer.

4 While the oil is heating, working 1 piece at a time, pull the cube steak from the milk and place in the cracker mixture. Cover all sides of the meat with the mixture, firmly pressing it to fully coat all the crevices. Set aside on a plate, and repeat with the remaining cube steaks.

5 Once the oil is hot and shimmering, working in batches, carefully place the breaded meat into the oil (dropping away from you) and fry for 3 to 5 minutes on each side, or until crispy golden brown and cooked through. Place the pieces on a wire rack in a rimmed baking sheet to drip dry.

6 Prepare the cream gravy. If the oil isn't burnt, pour out all but ½ cup from the cast-iron skillet to use for the gravy. (Otherwise, use butter.) Place over medium heat until hot.

7 Add the all-purpose flour, and whisk until the flour begins to brown, about 2 minutes. Then slowly add the whole milk, and whisk continuously until it begins to thicken and is smooth. Add more milk as needed to reach the desired consistency. Season to taste with salt and pepper.

8 Plate the chicken fried steak with gravy. It goes great with a side of mashed potatoes and green beans. Finish with freshly cracked black pepper, and enjoy!

PREP TIME:
**50 MINUTES +
24 HOURS TO CURE**

COOK TIME:
30–45 MINUTES

SERVES:
2–4

roasted chicken

A whole roasted chicken does not have to be a letdown. The age-old issue is if you cook a chicken whole, you're likely going to have to cook the breasts into the depths of the Sahara Desert before the legs even think about being cooked through. But with this method, you get a beautifully cooked whole chicken juicier than the ripest Texas peach with beautiful, crisp golden skin.

1 whole chicken
  (about 3 lb/1.5kg)
Kosher salt and freshly
  cracked black pepper,
  to taste
Seasonings of choice,
  to taste
Neutral-tasting oil,
  to coat

1 Spatchcock (butterfly) the chicken. Using kitchen shears, remove the entire backbone from the chicken by cutting along both sides of the spine until the spine can be removed in one piece. Turn the bird over, cut-side down, and press firmly on the breast to crack the breastbone and flatten the bird.

2 Pat the bird as dry as possible in every little crevice. Season very generously with salt and pepper and any other seasonings you desire. Rub the seasoning in, and make sure to get salt into all the crevices and the underside of the chicken.

3 Place the chicken skin-side up on a wire rack over a foil-lined baking sheet. Refrigerate, uncovered, for 24 hours to cure and dry.

4 Preheat the oven to 450°F (230°C). Remove the chicken from the refrigerator and let rest at room temperature for 30 minutes. Then coat with a light layer of neutral-tasting oil.

5 Cook on the wire rack over the baking sheet for 30 to 45 minutes, or until the skin is beautifully browned and crispy. Check the breast meat after 25 minutes; if the breast meat reaches 160°F (70°C), remove the legs by separating them from where the skin connects them to the breasts and remove the breast meat from the oven. Leave the legs in the oven until crispy and golden brown and the meat reaches 160°F (70°C).

6 Let the meat rest, uncovered, for 8 minutes before carving. For a beautiful presentation, plate with fresh herbs. Enjoy!

note: To make gravy for serving, after the chicken is cooked, deglaze the baking sheet with 1 cup (250ml) boiling water. In a medium pot, melt 1 tablespoon (14g) butter. Once melted, add 1 tablespoon (9g) all-purpose flour, constantly stirring until bubbly. Stir in the deglazing mixture. Cook until thickened.

MEAT

mom's pot roast

I'd like to call this the "family weekend meal crutch." By that I mean it's the number one choice I think everyone should be able to lean on when they want something special on the weekend that feeds a lot of mouths with relatively minimal effort. It's fantastic with mashed or roasted potatoes. My mom knew exactly what she was doing when she came up with this one. Love ya, Mom; thank you for this recipe!

4 lb (2kg) chuck roast
Kosher salt and freshly cracked black pepper, to season
2 tbsp (30ml) neutral-tasting oil
1 large yellow onion, quartered
5 cloves garlic, sliced
1 qt (1 liter) beef stock (see **basic stock out of anything, page 28**)
8 sprigs thyme
5 medium carrots, cut into 1½-inch (3.75-cm) sections

Gravy:
6 tbsp (84g) **unsalted butter (page 33)**
½ cup (75g) unbleached all-purpose flour
3½ cups (875ml) cooking liquid from the roast

1 Preheat the oven to 325°F (170°C). Season the roast generously with salt and pepper. Heat a 5- to 7-quart (4.75–6.5-liter) Dutch oven over medium-high heat. Once hot, add the oil. Once the oil is extremely hot, add the roast and sear for 2 to 3 minutes on each side, or until the roast is nicely browned on every side. Remove the roast and set on a plate to the side.

2 Add the onion, garlic cloves, and salt and pepper to taste. Sauté over medium-high heat until the garlic is fragrant and the onion is just beginning to soften. Add the broth, and as soon as it boils, immediately reduce the heat to low. Once gently simmering, lower in the roast. Add the thyme sprigs around the roast.

3 Cover, transfer to the oven, and braise for 1½ hours. Then add the carrots around the roast, cover, and cook for another 1 to 1½ hours, or until the meat is falling-apart tender.

4 Remove the roast and veggies to a platter, and cover with foil to keep warm. Discard the thyme stems. Reserve 3½ cups (875ml) cooking liquid.

5 To make the gravy, in a medium saucepan, melt the butter over medium heat. Whisk in the flour and cook, whisking constantly, for 45 seconds. Gradually whisk in the cooking liquid until the desired consistency is reached. (You may not use all of the reserved liquid.) Continue stirring until completely smooth and then remove from the heat. Enjoy the roast and veggies with a generous ladleful of gravy per serving.

PREP TIME:
10 MINUTES + OVERNIGHT TO MARINATE

COOK TIME:
2 HOURS 20 MINUTES

SERVES:
8–10

chashu

Chashu (a.k.a. Japanese braised pork belly) is, in my opinion, one of the most underrated cooked meats in the game, and I'm happy to introduce it to you if you've never heard of it. It could be used in the shoyu ramen recipe in this book (page 226), but it's a perfect standalone recipe as well. Chashu makes a beautiful sandwich; or when chilled, you could katsu-bread some chunks of it (page 151) and fry it; or you could just chop some up and add it to a bowl of steamed rice and veggies.

3–4 lb (1.5–2kg) pork belly, skin removed
2 tbsp (30ml) neutral-tasting oil
¾ cup (175ml) shoyu
1 cup (250ml) mirin
1 cup (250ml) sake
¼ cup (50g) granulated sugar
1 cup (250ml) filtered water
2-inch (5-cm) piece fresh ginger, peeled and roughly chopped
1 bunch of green onions, cut into 2-inch (5-cm) segments
1 shallot, peeled and halved

1 Lay the pork belly flat on a surface. Starting from the longest side, roll the pork belly tightly into a log. Use kitchen twine to fasten the rolled belly every few inches along the length of the pork belly; you should have a nicely secured and tight log.

2 In a large Dutch oven or heavy-bottomed pot, heat the oil over medium-high heat. Once the oil is nearly smoking, add the rolled pork belly and sear for 2 to 3 minutes on each side, or until nicely browned. Turn off the heat, and set the pork to the side on a plate or board.

3 In a medium bowl, whisk together the shoyu, mirin, sake, sugar, and water until thoroughly combined. Pour the mixture into the Dutch oven, and set over medium-high heat. Bring to a boil, and deglaze the pan by scraping up any fond (the deeply browned or caramelized bits from the meat) left in the bottom of the pan. As soon as the mixture begins to boil, reduce the heat to low and let gently simmer. Add the pork back in, and nestle the ginger, green onions, and shallot on either side of the pork.

4 Once the mixture returns to a simmer, cover with a lid, transfer to the oven, and braise, turning the pork every 15 minutes, for 1½ to 2 hours, or until the pork is very tender but not falling apart.

5 Remove the pork from the Dutch oven and set to the side. The braising liquid should have reduced to a nice sauce. Let the sauce and meat cool most of the way. Then place the meat in a large resealable or vacuum sealable bag. Cover with about 1 cup (250ml) of the cooking liquid, seal the bag, and refrigerate overnight to marinate.

6 The next day, your chashu is ready to use in whatever recipe you'd like. Remove the twine, slice the pork, and sear it in a pan before serving or adding to any recipe. Store in an airtight container in the refrigerator for up to 10 days.

PREP TIME:
20 MINUTES + OVERNIGHT TO MARINATE + MAKING DIPPING SAUCE (IF DESIRED)

COOK TIME:
25 MINUTES

SERVES:
2–4

chicken nuggets

These nuggets represent beauty in simplicity. I kept the ingredients here pretty low-key. You can absolutely add any array of spices you'd like, or keep it the way it is. This chicken nugget is as good as the technique you put into it. If you are an expert chicken bread-er, then you will find this chicken nugget to satisfy all your chicken dreams.

1 lb (450g) boneless, skinless chicken thighs
2 cups (500ml) buttermilk
1 tbsp (18g) kosher salt
High-heat oil (such as canola, avocado, vegetable, lard, etc.), for frying
Dipping sauce, such as **ultra-garlicky mayo (page 46), ranch dressing (page 48),** or **all-purpose barbecue sauce (page 43)**

Dredge:
2 cups (300g) unbleached all-purpose flour
1 tbsp (12g) smoked paprika
1½ tbsp (15g) ground white pepper
1 tsp (5g) dried oregano
1 tbsp (14g) garlic powder
1½ tbsp (27g) kosher salt

1 Cut the chicken thighs into about 1-inch (2.5-cm) bite-sized pieces, and place them into a bowl as you're working. Once you've cut all the chicken, add the buttermilk and salt. Stir to thoroughly coat the chicken and dissolve the salt. Refrigerate, covered, for at least 1 hour or overnight.

2 Fill a large deep cast-iron skillet or heavy-bottomed pot with about 2½ inches (6.25cm) oil. (Do not fill the pot more than three-quarters full.) Heat over medium heat until it reaches 350°F (180°C). Adjust the heat up and down to maintain that temperature.

3 While the oil is heating, in a medium bowl, whisk together all of the ingredients for the dredge until evenly combined. Line a baking sheet with a wire cooling rack.

4 Once the oil is to temperature, working in batches, remove the chicken from the marinade and toss in the dredge mixture, making sure to aggressively press the chicken into the dredge so there are no uncoated spots on the chicken at all. Once the chicken is fully coated, gently shake off the excess.

5 Working in 3 or 4 batches so the pot isn't overcrowded, fry the chicken pieces for 4 to 6 minutes, or until the chicken is a beautiful golden brown and cooked through to an internal temperature of 165°F (75°C). Once done, transfer the chicken to the wire cooling rack to drain. Repeat with the remaining chicken. Enjoy with any of your favorites sauces!

pastas & sandwiches

I don't know why we combined these two. Probably because they're both something I dream about.

PREP TIME:
5 MINUTES + MAKING PESTO SAUCE & GNOCCHI

COOK TIME:
1 MINUTE

SERVES:
4

pesto gnocchi

Gnocchi is often served with some type of butter or tomato sauce, but since you don't really see gnocchi that often, I always feel like it needs a sauce that's also not used often enough. I think the herbaceous, rich basil flavor combined with a gentle slap in the face of garlic goes beautifully with these voluptuous pillows. Yes, they're voluptuous.

Kosher salt and freshly cracked black pepper, to taste

1 batch uncooked **potato gnocchi (page 72)**

1 batch **pesto sauce (page 42)**

Freshly grated Parmigiano-Reggiano cheese, to serve

1 In a pot large enough to fit the batch of gnocchi, fill three-quarters full with water. Season the water very generously with salt (until it's about as salty as the ocean). Bring to a boil.

2 Add the gnocchi, and boil until all of them have floated to the top, about 1 minute. Remove the gnocchi to a medium bowl. Add a generous amount of the sauce plus 1 or 2 tablespoons (15 or 30ml) pasta water. Toss together until incorporated, and season to taste with salt.

3 Pile high into serving bowls, and finish each bowl with a nice, mountainous grating of Parmigiano-Reggiano and freshly cracked black pepper. Enjoy!

carbonara

It's hands down one of the simplest and best pasta dishes of all time. Somehow I have the ingredients on hand 95 percent of the time. The beauty is that all you actually need is pasta, cheese, and egg yolks to prepare the majority of what makes up the dish here. You can freestyle with whatever salty cured meats you might have in the fridge.

Kosher salt and freshly cracked black pepper, to taste

1 lb (450g) uncooked spaghetti (such as **fresh pasta, page 70**)

4 oz (110g) uncooked guanciale, pancetta, or bacon, diced into ½-inch (1.25-cm) cubes

2 cloves garlic, roughly chopped

5–6 large egg yolks

1¼ cups (310g) freshly grated Parmigiano-Reggiano or Grana Padano cheese, plus more to serve

½ cup (118g) freshly grated Pecorino Romano cheese

1 Bring a large pot of water seasoned very generously with salt to a boil. (It should be VERY salty—nearly as salty as the ocean.) Cook the spaghetti until al dente, about 4 minute for fresh pasta or 12 minutes for dried pasta. Once the pasta is cooked, reserve 1 cup (250ml) pasta water and drain the pasta.

2 While the pasta is cooking, in a large cold skillet, add the guanciale. Set the heat to medium-low, and cook, stirring occasionally, until the fat renders out and the guanciale is browned and crispy. Remove the skillet from the heat, and stir in the garlic.

3 Add the pasta to the pan with the meat and garlic. (The pan should be warm but not extremely hot; you won't use more heat.) Toss to coat.

4 Add the egg yolks, Parmigiano-Reggiano, and Pecorino Romano. Using tongs, toss together vigorously while drizzling in the reserved pasta water about 1 tablespoon (15ml) at a time to help melt the cheese and bring the mixture into a beautiful, glossy, emulsified sauce. You will likely use about ½ cup (125ml) pasta water total.

5 Plate and top with Parmigiano-Reggiano and freshly cracked black pepper. Enjoy immediately.

PASTAS & SANDWICHES

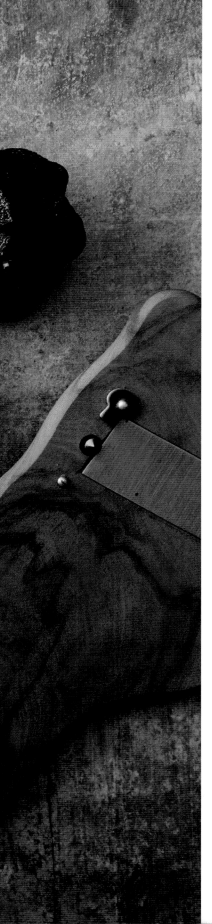

PREP TIME:
**5 MINUTES +
MAKING PASTA
(IF DESIRED)**

COOK TIME:
15 MINUTES

SERVES:
2

cacio e pepe

Yet another insanely simple pasta dish. Somehow the Italians have figured out the true beauty in simplicity within food. Essentially this is just cheese, pepper, salt, and pasta; and it creates a symphony of simple flavors that make Italian cuisine the king that it is.

Kosher salt, to season
½ lb (225g) uncooked bucatini or spaghetti (such as **fresh pasta, page 70**)
2 tbsp (30ml) extra-virgin olive oil
2 tsp (6g) freshly cracked coarse black pepper
1 cup (248g) freshly grated Parmigiano-Reggiano cheese, plus more to serve
½ cup (118g) freshly grated Pecorino Romano cheese
Freshly shaved black truffle (optional), to garnish

1 Bring a large pot of water seasoned very generously with salt to a boil. (It should be VERY salty—nearly as salty as the ocean.) Cook the pasta until just under al dente, about 1 minute for fresh pasta and 7 minutes for dried. Once the pasta is cooked, reserve 1½ cups (350ml) of the pasta water and drain the pasta.

2 In a medium saucepan, heat the olive oil over medium heat. Once hot, add the pepper and toast for about 30 seconds.

3 Add 1 cup (250ml) of the reserved pasta water. Bring to a simmer, and add the semi-cooked pasta to the saucepan. Let simmer vigorously for 3 to 5 minutes, or until the liquid is reduced by about 75 percent. (Add more of the reserved pasta liquid if the liquid reduces too fast.)

4 Add the Parmigiano-Reggiano and Pecorino Romano. Using tongs, mix and toss vigorously until all of the cheese is evenly distributed and melted and a creamy sauce has formed. Turn off the heat.

5 Transfer to a serving bowl, garnish with more freshly grated Parmigiano-Reggiano, and top with freshly shaved black truffle (if using). Enjoy!

cubanos

Yes, you've craved one since you saw the movie *Chef,* and yes, you can make them actually shockingly easily when you have some meat and bread to do it.

Unsalted butter **(page 33),** softened, to coat all sides

2 loaves **cubano bread (page 68),** sliced to form 4 sandwiches

2 lb (1kg) thin slices of boiled ham (not smoked)

Yellow mustard, to coat

4–6 **dill pickles (page 20),** thinly sliced lengthwise (about ¼ inch/0.5cm thick)

2–4 cups **mojo-braised pulled pork (page 146)**

8 slices Swiss cheese

1   Butter the inside of each slice of Cubano bread with butter. In a large cold pan, place the bread buttered-side down over medium heat. Toast.

2   While the bread toasts, in a separate medium pan, add a little butter and melt to coat the bottom. Working a few slices at a time, sear the ham over medium-high heat, browning both sides. Set the ham to the side and keep warm.

3   Once the bread is toasted, generously coat the inside of each slice with yellow mustard. On the bottom slice of each sandwich, arrange the sliced pickles to cover, followed by a stacked layer of the seared ham. Add a layer of pulled pork, and top with a generous amount of Swiss cheese. (I like to torch the cheese and get the melting started.) Place the tops of the bread on the sandwiches.

4   Preheat a heavy cast-iron pan (which you'll use to flatten the toasting sandwich). Generously coat the top and bottom of the sandwiches with butter. Working in batches, in a medium, cold pan, place the sandwiches and set over medium heat. Place the preheated heavy cast-iron pan on top to press into the bread. Toast the sandwich until the bottom is golden. Then flip it and place the cast-iron skillet back on top to toast the other side. Repeat the process to make the other sandwiches. (A panini press also works.)

5   Cut each sandwich on the diagonal into 2 pieces, and enjoy.

PASTAS & SANDWICHES

better than popeyes chicken sandwich

PREP TIME:
**1 HOUR + OVERNIGHT TO MARINATE +
MAKING PICKLES, BUTTER, BUNS, MAYO,
& HOT SAUCE (IF DESIRED)**

COOK TIME:
25 MINUTES

SERVES:
6

This is a very important recipe to me on many levels. I created it completely on a whim because I was distraught and annoyed by the level of insanity caused by the launch of the coveted fast-food sandwich...and I knew I could do much, much better. This is also a recipe that ultimately made me decide to launch the "But Better" series on my YouTube channel, which I love, and so do the many people who watch me.

6 large boneless, skinless chicken thighs (don't trim off fat; about ¾ lb/340g total)
High-heat oil (such as canola, avocado, vegetable, lard, etc.), for frying
6 large **dill pickles (page 20)**
Unsalted butter (page 33), for toasting
6 sandwich buns (see **my famous multipurpose dough, pages 60–63**)

Marinade:
2 cups (500ml) buttermilk
2 tsp (12g) kosher salt
2 tsp (7g) garlic powder
1 tsp (4g) serrano powder (or any spicy chili powder such as cayenne)

Flour mixture:
3 cups (450g) unbleached all-purpose flour
2½ tsp (15g) kosher salt
2 tsp (7g) garlic powder
1½ tsp (6g) smoked paprika
1 tsp (4g) oyster mushroom powder (optional)
½ tsp (2g) freshly cracked black pepper
1 tsp (4g) cayenne (optional; for heat)

Sauce:
¾ cup (173g) **mayonnaise (page 44)**
8 cloves black garlic, puréed or finely chopped (see note)
1 tbsp (15ml) **hot sauce (page 41)**
Kosher salt, to taste
1 tsp (5g) smoked paprika
Squeeze of fresh lemon juice, or to taste

1 Prepare the marinade. In a medium bowl, whisk together the buttermilk, salt, garlic powder, and serrano powder.

2 Add the chicken to the marinade, making sure the pieces are fully submerged. Cover with plastic wrap and refrigerate for at least 1 hour or overnight.

3 Prepare the flour mixture. In a large shallow baking dish, combine the all-purpose flour, salt, garlic powder, smoked paprika, oyster mushroom powder (if using), pepper, and cayenne (if you want it spicy). Whisk together until combined.

4 Fill a large deep cast-iron skillet or heavy-bottomed pot with about 2½ inches (6.25cm) oil. (Do not fill the pot more than three-quarters full.) Heat over medium heat until it reaches 350°F (180°C). Adjust the heat up and down to maintain that temperature.

5 While the oil is heating, drizzle 2 to 3 tablespoons (30–45ml) of the marinade into the flour mixture, and toss it around. (This gives you some extra-flaky bits on the chicken.)

6 Remove a piece of chicken from the marinade, coat it in the flour mixture, pressing very firmly into the chicken to make sure it's thoroughly coated, and shake off the excess flour. Set aside on a baking sheet, and repeat with the remaining chicken.

7 Working in batches so you don't overcrowd the pot, carefully place the breaded chicken into the oil (dropping away from you). Fry for 6 to 10 minutes while maintaining the 350°F (180°C) temperature. The chicken is done when it's golden brown and reaches an internal temperature of 165°F (75°C). Place on a wire rack in a rimmed baking sheet to drain and cool.

8 Make the sauce. In a medium bowl, mix together the mayonnaise, puréed black garlic, hot sauce, kosher salt, smoked paprika, and lemon juice until fully combined.

9 Slice the whole pickles lengthwise into ¼-inch- (0.5-cm-) thick slices.

10 To assemble, butter and toast the buns. Generously apply the spicy mayo on the bottom and top. Place a layer of the pickle slices on the bottom, followed by a chicken piece. Place the top bun, and enjoy.

note: You can find black garlic at most grocery stores or even Asian markets. Of course, as I always say...you can make it yourself, and I do have a guide on how to do that (if you're so ambitious) on my YouTube channel.

PREP TIME:
30 MINUTES + OVERNIGHT TO MARINATE + MAKING BISCUITS & BUTTER (IF DESIRED)

COOK TIME:
25 MINUTES

SERVES:
8

honey butter chicken biscuits

This time it's Texans eyeballing me. By that I mean, there is a certain restaurant that makes these for breakfast (and in my opinion it's just not a breakfast food)...and I think...well...mine is better. I'm sorry.

4 boneless, skinless chicken breasts (about 1½ lb/680g total)

High-heat oil (such as canola, avocado, vegetable, lard, etc.), for frying

Buttermilk biscuits (page 74; you can prepare these while the chicken marinates, just before cooking the chicken), hot or warmed

Marinade:
2 cups (500ml) buttermilk
½ tbsp (12g) gochujang (optional)
2 tsp (6g) white pepper
1 tbsp (8g) garlic powder
1 tbsp (8g) onion powder
1½ tsp (9g) kosher salt
1 tbsp (8g) smoked paprika

Dredge:
2 cups (300g) unbleached all-purpose flour
1 tbsp (18g) kosher salt
1 tsp (3g) smoked paprika
1 tbsp (8g) garlic powder
1 tbsp (8g) serrano powder (optional)
1½ tsp (1g) freshly cracked black pepper

Honey butter:
½ cup (160g) wildflower honey
1 tbsp (21g) avocado honey (optional; or use more wildflower honey)
6 sage leaves
3½ tbsp (49g) **salted butter (page 33)**

1 Prepare the marinade. In a large bowl, combine the buttermilk, gochujang (if using), white pepper, garlic powder, onion powder, salt, and smoked paprika. Whisk together until thoroughly combined.

2 Cut each chicken breast in half widthwise. Place the thicker halves between 2 pieces of plastic wrap and pound into an even thickness to match the thinner halves, ½ to ¾ inch (1.25–2cm) thick.

3 Place each piece of chicken into the buttermilk mixture, and cover with plastic wrap. Let marinate in the refrigerator for 1 hour or overnight. Make the buttermilk biscuits while the chicken marinates, just before cooking the chicken, so they're fresh.

4 Fill a large deep cast-iron skillet or heavy-bottomed pot with about 2½ inches (6.25cm) oil. (Do not fill the pot more than three-quarters full.) Heat over medium heat until it reaches 350°F (180°C). Adjust the heat up and down to maintain that temperature.

5 While the oil heats, prepare the dredge. In a medium bowl, whisk together the flour, salt, smoked paprika, garlic powder, serrano powder (if using), and pepper until combined.

6 Drizzle 2 to 3 tablespoons (30–45ml) of the marinade into the flour mixture, if desired, and toss it around. (This gives you some extra-flaky bits on the chicken.)

7 Working 1 piece at a time, remove the chicken from the buttermilk mixture, allowing the liquid to drip off. Place into the dredge, pressing very firmly into the chicken to make sure it's thoroughly coated, and shake off the excess. Set aside, and repeat with the remaining chicken.

8 Working 2 or 3 pieces at time so the skillet isn't overcrowded, carefully place the breaded chicken in the oil (dropping away from you), and fry for 5 to 7 minutes, or until golden brown. The chicken is done when it reaches an internal temperature of 165°F (75°C). Place on a wire rack in a rimmed baking sheet to drain.

9 Prepare the honey butter. In a small pot, combine the wildflower honey and avocado honey (if using) over medium heat, constantly whisking, until melted together. Once the honey is hot, turn off the heat and add the sage. Continue whisking constantly.

10 Whisk in the salted butter until fully emulsified into a smooth and thickened honey butter. Remove the sage leaves before serving.

11 Open each buttermilk biscuit, place a piece of chicken on the bottom, drizzle generously with the honey butter, and top with the other half of the biscuit. Enjoy!

PREP TIME:
**5 MINUTES +
MAKING MAYO &
BREAD (IF DESIRED)**

COOK TIME:
20 MINUTES

SERVES:
4

the perfect blt

Normally I want some *OOMPH* to my sandwich and always feel rather unsatisfied with a BLT. But this one, I promise you, will leave you so satisfied you'll have to lie down afterward.

16 slices uncooked
  thick-cut bacon
  (1/3 inch/0.75cm thick)
8–12 slices ripe tomato
  (½ inch/1.25cm thick)
Kosher salt and freshly
  cracked black pepper,
  to taste
6 tbsp (86g)
  **mayonnaise
  (page 44)**
6 tbsp (90g) Dijon
  mustard
8 slices **basic
  sourdough bread
  (page 54),** toasted
  (see note)
8 leaves butter lettuce

1 Line a baking sheet with foil, and arrange the bacon in an even layer on top. Place in a cold oven, and heat the oven to 425°F (220°C). Roast the bacon for 20 minutes, or until nicely browned and cooked through. Drain on paper towels.

2 While the bacon is cooking, season the tomato slices on both sides with salt and pepper. (This is crucial!)

3 In a small bowl, stir together the mayonnaise and mustard until combined.

4 To assemble the sandwiches, spread the desired amount of Dijon-mayo sauce on all slices of the toast. For each sandwich, layer on the lettuce (folding it to fit the shape of the bread), the seasoned tomato slices, and finally the bacon. Hit the top of the bacon with freshly cracked black pepper to taste.

5 Close the sandwiches, cut on the diagonal, and enjoy!

note: You can either toast your bread dry in a toaster or in a pan with butter. Personally, I prefer to toast mine in a pan with butter...better flavor and texture.

189

PREP TIME:
**2 MINUTES + MAKING BREAD & BUTTER
(IF DESIRED)**

COOK TIME:
8 MINUTES

SERVES:
1

grilled cheese

We are using salted butter in this recipe because it is the right thing to do. We will have salty goodness EMBEDDED into every bite of the beautiful golden crust. It's a beauty-in-simplicity kinda thing. It's amazing with tomato soup (page 229).

2 tsp (10g) whole-grain mustard

2 slices country-style bread or **basic sourdough bread (page 54)**

2 slices Monterey Jack cheese

2 slices smoked Gouda cheese

2 tbsp (28g) **salted butter (page 33)**, softened

1 Spread the mustard on each slice of the bread. Then layer your Monterey Jack and Gouda onto 1 of the slices. Close the sandwich.

2 Butter the outside of each slice of bread.

3 Place the sandwich in a small cold pan over medium heat. Cook until the bottom is deeply golden brown, 2 to 4 minutes. (Never flip early!) Then flip the sandwich and toast the other side until crispy golden brown and the cheese is fully melted.

4 Remove from the pan, and slice on the diagonal (because for some reason that makes it taste better). Enjoy!

PREP TIME:
10 MINUTES + MAKING BREAD, STEAK, & MAYO (IF DESIRED)

COOK TIME:
10 MINUTES

SERVES:
4

steak sandwiches

I've always loved steak sandwiches but never ate them often. Usually I'd find cuts of beef in there that were so chewy they ruined it for me. That's when I thought to myself, "You know what? Why not take it into my own hands and use a really beautifully cooked nice cut of steak and make this into the steak sandwich I WISH I could go out and get?"

2 tbsp (30ml) neutral-tasting oil

1 large sweet onion, cut into ½-inch (1.25-cm) rings (keep the rings intact)

2 large tomatoes, cut into about 8 (¼–½-inch/0.5–1.25-cm) slices

Kosher salt and freshly cracked black pepper, to taste

8 slices **basic sourdough bread (page 54),** toasted

2 large steaks (1 lb/450g each; see **the perfect steak, page 144**), cooked as desired, sliced ½ inch (1.25cm) thick, hot or cold

8 slices Gruyère cheese

Sauce:
¾ cup (173g) **mayonnaise (page 44)**

3 tbsp (45g) whole-grain mustard

2 cloves garlic, grated

2 tsp (10g) freshly grated horseradish (optional)

Kosher salt and freshly cracked black pepper, to taste

1 Prepare the sauce. In a small bowl, stir together the mayonnaise, whole-grain mustard, garlic, and horseradish (if using) until thoroughly combined. Season with salt and pepper to taste, and stir to incorporate.

2 In a large skillet, heat the oil over medium-high heat. Once the oil is very hot and nearly smoking, add the sliced sweet onion in a single layer. (Cook the onion in batches if needed.) Let the onion slices sear for 2 to 3 minutes, or until deeply cooked on one side. Then flip and sear the other side for another 2 to 3 minutes. Remove from the heat and set aside.

3 Season the tomato slices on both sides with salt and pepper, and let them rest for 2 minutes. (This is a crucial step to having any perfect sandwich.)

4 Preheat the broiler. On a baking sheet, assemble each sandwich. Add as much sauce as desired on all slices of the toasted bread. Layer on the seasoned tomatoes, the sliced steak, the seared onion rings, and finally the slices of cheese. Before adding the top slice of bread, pop the sandwiches under the broiler just until the cheese is melted. Remove from the oven and immediately top with your other sauced, sliced bread.

5 Serve sandwiches sliced in half or whole, and enjoy!

PREP TIME:
**25 MINUTES + MAKING BUTTER, BUNS,
PICKLES, MAYO, & HOT SAUCE (IF DESIRED)**

COOK TIME:
20 MINUTES

SERVES:
4

smash burgers

A true testament to a great cook isn't just how perfectly they execute a classic omelet or how flawlessly they emulsify a sauce, but also how well they build a burger—it takes a deep, committed understanding of the sandwich holding and eating experience. Are the toppings going to slip out from under you when you take a bite? Is it too dry because you didn't have enough fat in the beef? These are important questions, folks.

2 tbsp (30ml) neutral-tasting oil

1 large sweet onion, sliced into thick rounds

Kosher salt, to taste

1 lb (450g) ground beef (70–80% lean; double for ½ lb/225g burgers)

8 slices of cheese (such as Gouda, cheddar, or pepper jack)

4 tbsp (56g) **unsalted butter (page 33)**

4 burger buns (see **my famous multipurpose dough, pages 60–63**)

1–2 heirloom tomatoes, sliced ¼ inch (0.5cm) thick

2 **dill pickles (page 20),** sliced lengthwise

½ head iceberg lettuce, thinly sliced

Mustard sauce:

½ cup (115g) **mayonnaise (page 44)**

2 tbsp (30g) whole-grain mustard

½ bunch of finely sliced chives

1 clove garlic, grated

1 tbsp (15ml) **hot sauce (page 41;** optional)

Kosher salt and freshly cracked black pepper, to taste

1 In a 10-inch (25-cm) skillet, heat the oil over medium-high heat. Once very hot and the oil begins to move around the pan, add the sliced onion. Season generously with salt. Cook, stirring often, until the onions are cooked and lightly charred. Set aside in a bowl to cool.

2 Prepare the mustard sauce. In a small bowl, mix together all of the ingredients. Cover with plastic wrap, and refrigerate until ready to use.

3 Portion the ground beef into 4 even balls (4 oz/110g each). Heat a large, dry cast-iron skillet over medium-high heat. Once the pan is hot, place the beef balls in the skillet, spacing them apart as much as you can, working in batches if needed. Smash them with a spatula to form flat patties about ½ inch (1.25cm) thick. Season the tops generously with salt to taste. Let the patties sear for about 3 minutes, or until you get a nice crust on the bottom. Flip the patties, season the other side with salt, and sear for another 3 to 4 minutes, or until the patties are fully cooked through and nicely browned on the bottom.

4 Add 2 slices of cheese on top of each patty in the pan. Add a small splash of water to the pan to create steam, and immediately cover with a lid or foil. Steam until the cheese is fully melted and then uncover and remove from the heat.

5 Spread the butter generously over the cut sides of the buns. In a large dry pan or on a griddle, toast all of the buns cut-side down over medium heat until beautifully browned.

6 Season the tomato slices on both sides with salt, and let them rest for 2 minutes.

7 Assemble the burgers. On the bottom buns, spread out a dollop of the mustard sauce, followed by a layer of sliced tomatoes, pickle slices, iceberg lettuce, and a beef patty. Top the patties with charred onions and another generous dollop of the sauce. Finally, place the top bun. Enjoy immediately.

vegetables & salads

The only reason anyone is picky with the vegetables they eat is that most of the time they're cooked terribly. No more of that. Vegetables are f—ing awesome when you give them the love they deserve.

fried brussels sprouts

A lot of restaurants really mess this up—either the brussels sprouts are almost completely raw and soaked in hot oil, or they are incredibly underseasoned and bland. When executed properly and dressed in a nice sauce, brussels sprouts become one of the best vegetable dishes in the world. Because I happened to work at the restaurant that basically invented them, I figured this would be a nice homage. Shout-out to Uchiko and one of the Tempura Kings, Dan the Man.

½ cup plus 2 tbsp (125g) granulated sugar
½ cup (125ml) white distilled vinegar
½ cup (125ml) soy sauce
¼ cup (60ml) fish sauce
¼ cup (60ml) fresh orange juice
2-inch (5-cm) piece fresh ginger, peeled and grated
2 fresh Thai or serrano chilies, thinly sliced
1½ tbsp (11g) cornstarch
1½ tbsp (25ml) filtered water
4 cloves garlic, finely chopped
High-heat oil (such as canola, avocado, vegetable, lard, etc.), for frying
1 lb (450g) brussels sprouts, halved (or quartered if very large)
Kosher salt, to taste
Fresh lemon juice, to taste

1 In a medium saucepan, combine the sugar, vinegar, soy sauce, fish sauce, orange juice, ginger, and chilies. Place the pot over medium-high heat, and cook, stirring occasionally, until it reaches a boil. Boil for 3 to 5 minutes.

2 While the sauce is boiling, in a small bowl, whisk together the cornstarch and water to create a slurry.

3 Whisk the cornstarch slurry into the boiling sauce and allow to boil for another 1 to 2 minutes, or until the sauce is thickened. Remove from the heat, and stir in the garlic. Let steep for 5 minutes in the hot sauce, strain the sauce, and discard the solids.

4 In a large deep cast-iron skillet or heavy-bottomed pot, fill just over halfway, or about 2½ inches (6.25cm), with oil. Heat the oil over medium heat until it reaches 350°F (180°C). Adjust the heat up and down to maintain that temperature.

5 Carefully (they usually spit a little bit when added to the oil) add about 1 cup brussels sprouts at once to the oil. Let fry for about 7 minutes, or until beautifully browned, crispy, and cooked through. Immediately remove from the oil using a kitchen spider or slotted spoon, and place in a heatproof bowl. Work in batches to fry all of the remaining brussels sprouts.

6 In a serving bowl, dress the fried brussels sprouts with a generous amount of sauce, season lightly with salt, and add a small squeeze of lemon juice. Enjoy!

VEGETABLES & SALADS

charred kale

Let me say this carefully: I hate kale. Well...I hate kale in most contexts. If you're in the same boat, this one will be a true revelation. Either that, or you love kale and you didn't realize it could be taken to such heights.

2 tbsp (30ml) extra-virgin olive oil, plus more if needed
2 bunches of kale, stems and ribs removed
2 cloves garlic, peeled
Zest and juice of 1 lemon, divided
Kosher salt and freshly cracked black pepper, to taste
Freshly shaved Parmigiano-Reggiano cheese, to serve

1 In a large skillet, heat the olive oil over medium-high heat. Once the pan is extremely hot, add the first batch of kale. You don't want to stack it; arrange in a single even layer.

2 Let the kale sear, undisturbed, for 1 to 2 minutes, or until it begins to slightly char. Toss the pan and continue to sear for 3 to 4 minutes more, or until the kale is wilted and charred on both sides.

3 Remove the charred kale to a bowl, and repeat in batches until you've cooked all of the kale, adding more oil to the pan as needed.

4 While the kale is still hot, grate in the garlic. Add the lemon juice, and season to taste with salt and pepper. Toss together. Taste and adjust the salt levels.

5 Place the kale on serving plates. Garnish with the lemon zest. Finish it off with some freshly shaved Parmigiano-Reggiano. Drizzle with olive oil (if desired), and enjoy.

broccolini with toasted peanuts & chili oil

Look, I'm not trying to convert anyone by fancifying a vegetable. The only point I'm trying to make with this is that almost every vegetable tastes incredible when roasted.

½ cup (75g) raw peanuts
2 bunches of Broccolini
2½ tbsp (40ml) extra-
   virgin olive oil
Kosher salt and freshly
   cracked black pepper,
   to taste
2 tbsp (30ml) chili oil
Zest and juice of 1 lime
Thinly sliced fresh
   serrano chilies
   (optional), for garnish
Flaky sea salt,
   for garnish

1 Preheat the oven to 375°F (190°C). Spread out the peanuts on a baking sheet lined with parchment paper. Toast the peanuts for 8 minutes, or until they are deeply toasted. Let them cool completely, place them in a bag, and crush into medium-coarse crumbs.

2 Increase the oven temperature to 400°F (200°C). In a medium bowl, toss together the Broccolini, olive oil, and salt and pepper to taste. Arrange the coated Broccolini on a baking sheet lined with parchment paper. Roast for 15 minutes, or until al dente and lightly charred on the florets.

3 Place the Broccolini on a serving plate, and drizzle with the chili oil and lime juice to taste. Top with lime zest and serrano chili slices (if using). Sprinkle on the crushed roasted peanuts and flaky salt. Enjoy!

VEGETABLES & SALADS

PREP TIME:
10 MINUTES + MAKING MAYO, HOT SAUCE, & PICKLES (IF DESIRED)

COOK TIME:
10 MINUTES

SERVES:
4

esquites

Elote is one of the greatest foods on the planet. Is this elote (a.k.a. grilled corn on the cob)? Before anyone gets mad...no, not exactly. It's also not really ultra-traditional esquites (sautéed corn in a bowl). While this dish suffers a little bit from an identity crisis, you'll find it reminiscent of elote but served beautifully in a bowl and ready to be devoured with a spoon.

4 medium ears corn (shucked)
3 tbsp (45ml) **addicting spicy mayo (page 46)**
Kosher salt, to taste
2 tsp (5g) smoked paprika
Juice of ½ lime
Hot sauce (page 41), to serve
Pickled red onions (see **pickled anything, page 20**), to serve
Diced avocado, to serve
Thinly sliced fresh serrano chilies, to serve
Freshly grated aged Manchego cheese, to serve
Cilantro leaves, for garnish

1 Grill all sides of the ears of corn until a light char develops and the kernels are still crunchy and moist. Once grilled, using a knife, remove all of the kernels from the cobs into a large bowl.

2 Into the same bowl, add the addicting spicy mayo, salt to taste, smoked paprika, and lime juice. Stir together until fully incorporated.

3 Spoon the corn mixture into a serving bowl. Top with a drizzle of hot sauce, pickled red onions, diced avocado, and thinly sliced serrano chilies.

4 Top with freshly grated aged Manchego, garnish with cilantro leaves, and serve.

the greatest caesar salad of your life

It bothers me to no end knowing there are innocent people lifting forks of Caesar salad to their mouths soaked in improperly made Caesar dressing (which, let me tell you, could be astronomically better). Traditionally, you'd use olive oil and maybe Worcestershire sauce, but I've created a more versatile version that still maintains the very essence of what makes a proper Caesar salad taste incredible.

1 head romaine, coarsely chopped
Kosher salt and freshly cracked black pepper, to taste
Freshly shaved Parmigiano-Reggiano cheese, to serve

Croutons:
½ loaf **basic sourdough bread (page 54),** cut into 1-inch (2.5-cm) cubes
⅓ cup (75g) **unsalted butter (page 33),** melted
2 cloves garlic, grated
Freshly cracked black pepper, to taste
Flaky sea salt, to taste

Dressing:
5 cloves garlic
½ tsp (3g) kosher salt
3 anchovy fillets
1 large egg yolk
2 tsp (10g) Dijon mustard
Juice of 1 lemon, plus more to season
⅔ cup (150ml) neutral-tasting oil
½ cup (40g) freshly shaved Parmigiano-Reggiano cheese

1   Prepare the croutons. Preheat the oven to 350°F (180°C). In a large bowl, toss together all of the ingredients. Arrange the croutons in an even layer on a large baking sheet. Bake for about 20 minutes, or until nice and crispy, stirring occasionally so they brown evenly.

2   While the croutons are cooking, prepare the dressing. On a cutting board, smash the garlic cloves with the flat part of a knife. Generously sprinkle salt (which acts as an abrasive) over the garlic and anchovies. Finely chop the garlic and anchovies, smear with the flat side of the knife, and fold over itself. Continue to chop, smear, and fold until it becomes a paste.

3   In a small bowl, add the egg yolk. Whisk in the anchovy-garlic paste, along with the mustard and lemon juice. While constantly whisking, add the oil in a very slow, steady stream until emulsified. Whisk in the Parmigiano-Reggiano. Taste and season with more lemon juice and salt. (This makes enough for about 8 servings. Store remaining dressing in an airtight container in the refrigerator for up to 1 week.)

4   In a large bowl, season the romaine lightly with salt, and toss with dressing to your liking. Portion onto serving plates. Finish each plate of salad with croutons, freshly shaved Parmigiano-Reggiano, and freshly cracked black pepper. Taste and adjust salt levels, if desired. Enjoy!

PREP TIME:
25 MINUTES + MAKING CHICKEN, EGGS, & CHÈVRE (IF DESIRED)

SERVES:
2–4

cobb salad

Let it be known that I absolutely love a Cobb salad, but as I've stated many times (on camera, in person, and generally throughout my life), I thoroughly dislike bleu cheese. Don't get me wrong—I love stinky funky cheeses and foods that many find revolting, but bleu cheese is not one of them. That's why this Cobb salad is full of all the iconic flavors you want, sans bleu cheese. Feel free to add it if you wanna make me sad.

1 head romaine, coarsely chopped

1 head Boston lettuce, coarsely chopped

2 chicken breasts (such as **chicken breasts that are actually good, page 156**), cooked and cubed or shredded

4 **perfect soft-boiled eggs (page 90),** diced

1 cup (150g) grape tomatoes, halved

8 slices cooked bacon, chopped

1 cup (112g) crumbled **chèvre (page 38)**

2 avocados, diced

½ bunch of chives (optional), very finely chopped

Dressing:

2½ tbsp (38g) Dijon mustard

⅓ cup (75ml) red wine vinegar

1 shallot, finely diced

1 clove garlic, grated

½ cup (125ml) extra-virgin olive oil

Kosher salt and freshly cracked black pepper, to taste

1 Prepare the dressing. In a small bowl, whisk together the mustard, vinegar, shallot, and grated garlic until combined. While continuously whisking, slowly drizzle in the olive oil until all of it is added and you have an emulsified dressing. Season to taste with salt and pepper.

2 Assemble each salad on serving plates by arranging single rows of each ingredient: romaine and Boston lettuce, chicken, egg, grape tomato halves, bacon bits, chèvre, and diced avocado. Garnish with chives (if using), drizzle with dressing, and enjoy! Store leftover dressing in an airtight container in the refrigerator for up to 1 week.

PREP TIME:
15 MINUTES + MAKING DRESSING, CHÈVRE, & PICKLES (IF DESIRED)

COOK TIME:
15 MINUTES

SERVES:
4

a respectable wedge salad

My first thought when I saw a wedge salad as a kid was, "This is some sort of ancient alien pyramid shape of lettuce that's been doused in an egregious amount of unidentifiable dressing." Obviously, there is a way to make this thing tasty and equally beautiful, too. In an effort to correct the experiences of my childhood, we'll begin with this wedge salad. Oh, and for those of you who've probably gasped by now about the lack of bleu cheese dressing, please understand that I hate it. Thank you...that is all.

2 tbsp (30ml) extra-virgin olive oil
1 cup (150g) grape tomatoes
4 slices prosciutto
1 head iceberg lettuce
1¼ cups (310ml) **ranch dressing (page 48)**
1 cup (112g) crumbled **chèvre (page 38)**
1 **dill pickle (page 20),** finely diced
½ bunch of chives, thinly sliced
Dill, for garnish
Freshly cracked black pepper, to taste

1   In a medium pan, heat the olive oil over medium-high heat. Once the pan is very hot, add the whole grape tomatoes. Sear, undisturbed, for 2 minutes. Then toss the pan and continue to sauté over medium-high heat until the tomatoes begin to deflate and soften but still hold their shape. Remove from the pan and set aside.

2   Reduce the heat to medium. In the same pan, arrange the prosciutto in a single layer. (You'll likely need to cook this in 2 batches.) Heat the pan over medium heat, and cook, flipping occasionally, until the prosciutto is completely crisp and nicely browned. Repeat for another batch, as needed. Crumble and set aside.

3   Discard the outer layer of leaves from the iceberg lettuce. Using the stem of the lettuce as the center point, cut the head into quarters, leaving a piece of the stem attached to each quarter so the sections don't fall apart.

4   To assemble, place a lettuce quarter on each serving plate, standing upright. Dress each generously with ranch dressing. Top with seared tomatoes, crumbled prosciutto, chèvre, dill pickle, chives, dill, and pepper. Enjoy!

soup

Underrated and underappreciated. I'm talking about soup.

PREP TIME:
30 MINUTES + MAKING STOCK (IF DESIRED)

COOK TIME:
1 HOUR 10 MINUTES

SERVES:
10

mom's chicken noodle soup

I mean, come on...you have to show respect to the mom. This stuff got me through sick days, and it warmed me up over the winter. It's also so good that you could easily eat this stuff year round. For the record, I added the herbs, but this is usually done very simply and is perfectly delicious without them.

2 medium carrots, cut into ½-inch (1.25-cm) rounds

2 medium yellow onions, roughly chopped

2 medium ribs celery, cut into ½-inch (1.25-cm) pieces

½ bunch of thyme

2 sprigs sage

3 bay leaves

1 (3–4 lb/1.5–2kg) whole chicken

3 qt (3 liters) chicken stock (see **basic stock out of anything, page 28;** see note), divided

12 oz (340g) uncooked egg noodles

Kosher salt and freshly cracked black pepper, to taste

Fresh torn or chopped herbs, such as flat-leaf parsley or basil leaves, to serve

1 In a 6- or 7-quart (5.5–6.5-liter) stockpot, add the carrots, onions, celery, thyme, sage, and bay leaves. Lay the whole chicken on top of the vegetables. Cover with 1 quart (1 liter) of the chicken stock.

2 Place over medium-high heat, and bring to a boil. Reduce the heat to low, cover, and very gently simmer for 1 hour, or until the chicken is falling apart.

3 Remove the chicken, thyme stems, sage, and bay leaves from the pot. Discard the herbs. Once the chicken is cool enough to handle, debone the chicken completely. Shred the meat and place back into the pot.

4 In a separate medium pot, bring the remaining 2 quarts (2 liters) chicken stock to a boil and add the egg noodles. Cook according to the package instructions, or until al dente.

5 Pour the noodle and broth mixture into the chicken pot. Mix together and season generously with salt and pepper.

6 To serve, ladle into bowls and top with fresh torn or chopped herbs of your choice. Enjoy.

note: If you use store-bought chicken stock, you're losing at least 50 percent of the flavor. I highly recommend using homemade chicken stock to make this as incredible as it should be.

PREP TIME:
40 MINUTES + MAKING STOCK (IF DESIRED)

COOK TIME:
1 HOUR

SERVES:
4

roasted mushroom soup with garlic chantilly cream

This is essentially a significantly upgraded version of that childhood favorite, cream of mushroom soup. It's what cream of mushroom should have been all along, but alas we must do it ourselves if we want greatness from our mushrooms. Be sure to grab the freshest, most beautiful mushrooms you can for this. Although they'll be blended, the fresher they are, the more intense their flavor will be.

1¾ cups (425ml) boiling filtered water
2 oz (55g) dried mushrooms (porcini, shiitake, or oyster)
2 lb (1kg) trumpet mushrooms (or any mix of your preferred mushrooms)
6 tbsp (90ml) neutral-tasting oil, divided
1 small yellow onion, roughly chopped
Kosher salt, to taste
3 cloves garlic, sliced
¼ cup (60ml) dry sherry
1½ cups (350ml) chicken stock (see **basic stock out of anything, page 28**)
¼ cup (60ml) extra-virgin olive oil
Sherry vinegar, to taste
Freshly cracked black pepper, to serve
Microgreens or herbs of choice (optional), to serve

Garlic chantilly cream:
1 cup (250ml) heavy whipping cream
1 tsp (6g) kosher salt
1 clove garlic, grated

1 Preheat the oven to 450°F (230°C). In a small metal bowl, pour the boiling water over the dried mushrooms. Cover with plastic wrap or foil and let steep for 15 minutes, or until the mushrooms are fully softened and cool enough to handle. Remove the mushrooms and squeeze them out over the water to catch excess liquid. Slice the mushrooms. Reserve both the liquid and the mushrooms separately.

2 Cut off the tough parts (if any) of the trumpet mushroom stems. Slice the trumpet mushrooms in half. With the tip of a paring knife, score the cut sides of each mushroom half in a small crosshatched pattern. In a medium bowl, toss the trumpet mushrooms with 3 tablespoons (45ml) neutral-tasting oil to coat evenly and thoroughly, using extra oil if needed to coat. On a rimmed baking sheet, arrange the mushrooms cut-side up. Roast for 20 to 25 minutes, or until the mushrooms are a deep golden brown. Reserve 4 to 8 of the largest mushroom halves for serving.

3 In a medium pot, heat the remaining 3 tablespoons (45ml) neutral-tasting oil over medium heat until shimmering and hot. Add the onion and season with salt to taste. Heat for 3 minutes, stirring occasionally, until the onion begins to soften.

217

4 Add the sliced garlic, and cook for an additional 30 seconds, or just until fragrant. Add the roasted trumpet mushrooms and rehydrated sliced mushrooms to the pot. Cook for 1 minute.

5 Increase the heat to medium-high, and add the dry sherry. Boil the mixture until it's almost completely evaporated. Then add all of the reserved mushroom rehydration liquid and the chicken stock. Bring to a boil, reduce the heat to low, and simmer, partially covered, for 30 minutes, or until all of the vegetables are extremely soft. (Well...technically mushrooms are fungi, but we can chat about that some other time.)

6 Place a strainer over a medium bowl, and strain the vegetables through a fine-mesh strainer to separate them from the liquid. Add all of the vegetables to a blender. Blend on high speed, adding the reserved liquid a little bit at a time, until the vegetables are loosened and blending in a vortex and the mixture is very smooth. Then, while blending, slowly stream in the olive oil. Season to taste with salt and a small splash of sherry vinegar.

7 Before serving, make the garlic Chantilly cream. In a medium bowl, using a handheld mixer on medium speed or a good old-fashioned whisk, beat the heavy whipping cream. When the cream starts to thicken, add the salt and continue beating until it forms soft peaks. Fold in the grated garlic.

8 To serve, pour the soup into 4 shallow serving bowls. To each bowl, add a dollop of the garlic Chantilly cream. Add 1 or 2 of the mushroom halves. Finish with freshly cracked black pepper. Top with microgreens or herbs (if using). Enjoy!

PREP TIME:
20 MINUTES + MAKING BUTTER & BROTH (IF DESIRED)

COOK TIME:
2 HOURS 10 MINUTES

SERVES:
7

french onion soup

This is the soup that calls your name as soon as the weather turns cold (or it does mine, at least). It's a perfect food, in my opinion. Sweet caramelized onions, rich beef stock, crunchy bread, melty cheese—everything you could want in a single sip of soup.

3½ lb (1.5kg) Vidalia onions (5–6 large)

5 tbsp (70g) **unsalted butter (page 33),** divided

1 tbsp (15ml) extra-virgin olive oil, plus more for brushing

Kosher salt and freshly cracked black pepper, to taste

2 tbsp (30ml) bourbon (optional)

1¼ cups (310ml) white wine

1½ qt (1.5 liters) beef stock (see **basic stock out of anything, page 28**)

10 sprigs thyme, tied together with kitchen twine

3 tbsp (45ml) dry sherry (optional)

7 oz (200g) Gruyère cheese

7 oz (200g) Gouda cheese

Baguette or other crusty bread, cut into ½–1-inch (1.25–2.5-cm) slices, to serve (2 slices per person)

1 Cut off and discard the tops and bottoms of the Vidalia onions. Cut in half, peel, and slice thinly across the grain. (See the photos on page 220.)

2 In a 6- to 8-quart (5.5–7.5-liter) stockpot, add 3 tablespoons (42g) butter and the olive oil. Heat over medium heat.

3 Once the butter begins to bubble, add the sliced onions. Season with salt, and stir to coat the onions with the butter and disperse the salt.

4 To caramelize, cook the onions over medium heat, stirring frequently and gently, for 45 to 90 minutes. Adjust the heat between medium and low as needed. If the onions start to stick, add a splash of water to loosen. The longer the onions cook, the softer they get, so start to fold them instead of stirring to prevent the onions from becoming mushy. Once the onions reach a very dark brown, they are finished.

5 After the onions are cooked, pour in the bourbon (if using). Let it boil and reduce the liquid until there is barely any bourbon left, about 2 minutes. Then add the white wine and bring to boil over high heat. Boil for 3 to 5 minutes, or until reduced by about 75 percent.

6 Add the beef stock, and bring to a simmer. Add the thyme bundle to the pot. Let simmer for 20 to 30 minutes, or until slightly reduced and slightly thickened.

7 Add the dry sherry (if using) and let simmer for an additional 1 to 2 minutes to cook off the alcohol.

8 Remove the pot from the heat, remove the bundle of thyme, and stir in the remaining 2 tablespoons (28g) butter, mixing together until completely melted. Season to taste with salt and pepper.

9 Preheat the oven to 425°F (220°C). Grate the Gruyère and Gouda, and toss the shreds together. Brush the baguette slices with olive oil. Bake the slices for 5 to 7 minutes, or until crispy but not browned. Remove the bread and then preheat the broiler to high.

10 If using ovenproof bowls, ladle in the soup, leaving ¼ inch (0.5cm) of space at the top. Top each with 2 slices of baguette bread, and sprinkle generously with the cheese. Broil for 2 to 3 minutes, or until melted and slightly browned. Serve and enjoy.

11 If using non-ovenproof bowls, top the individual toasts with the shredded cheese and broil on a foil-lined baking sheet until the cheese fully melts. Ladle soup into the bowls, and add the cheesy toast on top or to the side. Serve and enjoy.

Caramelizing onions, steps 1 to 4

PREP TIME:
**15 MINUTES + MAKING PHO BROTH/
CHUCK ROAST & MARROW**

COOK TIME:
20 MINUTES

SERVES:
4

beef pho

"Is pho or ramen better?" Look, I don't like these kinds of questions. They're a little too spiteful, in my opinion. I know you want to force me into answering this, so the best thing I can say is that when the mood strikes for pho, that's exactly what you're getting. And it's gotta be real, real good—like sweating profusely, take off your shirt, and cry while you eat it type good.

1 lb (450g) flank steak (uncooked)

Cooked chuck roast and marrow from **pho broth (page 30)**

2 qt (2 liters) **pho broth (page 30)**

8 oz (225g) uncooked rice noodles

½ large sweet onion, thinly sliced

1 Thai chili, thinly sliced

Handful of Thai basil leaves (see note)

Handful of cilantro leaves

Handful of mint leaves (optional)

2 limes, halved

Chili sauce

Hoisin sauce

1 Prepare the ingredients for serving. As thinly as possible, slice the flank steak across the grain. (You can freeze the steak for 10 to 15 minutes before cutting to make this easier.) Thinly slice the cooked (chilled) chuck roast. Bring the broth to a boil.

2 While the broth is heating, cook the rice noodles in a separate pot of water according to the package instructions. Rinse the cooked noodles well under warm water.

3 In 4 individual serving bowls, place the noodles in the bottom. Add the raw flank steak, the cooked chuck roast, and any reserved marrow.

4 Then pour in the boiling hot broth. Top with sliced onions, sliced chilies, Thai basil, cilantro, mint leaves (if using), and lime halves. Enjoy with chili sauce and hoisin sauce on the side.

note: If you can't find Thai basil, substitute regular basil.

SOUP

222

PREP TIME:
15 MINUTES + MAKING BUTTER, STOCK, & CHICKEN (IF DESIRED)

COOK TIME:
1 HOUR 20 MINUTES

SERVES:
4

chicken tortilla soup

If you don't love tortilla soup, you either have never had a good one, or you don't like tortillas. The crunch, the cheesiness, the toasty corn flavor, the tart yet slightly sweet tomatoes...this soup hits all the notes and is ripe for cracking open a cold one with the homies when served.

4 slices uncooked smoky bacon, chopped
1 tbsp (14g) **unsalted butter (page 33)**
1 medium yellow onion, roughly chopped
4 cloves garlic
2 jalapeños, seeded (if desired) and thinly sliced
1 tbsp (7g) smoked paprika
1½ tsp (3g) ground cumin
1 (14 oz/400g) can crushed tomatoes
3 cups (750ml) chicken stock (see **basic stock out of anything, page 28**)
1 tbsp (3g) finely chopped oregano
1½ cups (170g) fresh corn kernels
1 (14 oz/400g) can black beans, drained
3 roasted chicken breasts (such as **chicken breasts that are actually good, page 156** or **roasted chicken, page 162**), shredded
Kosher salt and freshly cracked black pepper, to taste

Options for topping:
Tortilla chips, crushed
1 avocado, diced
1½ cups (168g) shredded cheddar cheese
1 cup (246g) sour cream
Lime halves or wedges
Cilantro

1 Add the chopped bacon to a cold stockpot. Cook over medium heat for 5 to 10 minutes, or until the bacon is browned and crispy. With a slotted spoon, remove the bacon bits to a paper towel–lined plate to drain. Crumble until very fine.

2 Add the butter to the pot with the bacon fat. Once melted, add the onion. Cook for about 3 minutes, or until translucent. Then add the garlic and jalapeños, and cook for about 1 minute, or until fragrant.

3 Stir in the paprika and cumin to coat, and let cook for about 30 seconds.

4 Stir in the crushed tomatoes with their juice and the chicken stock. Bring to a boil, reduce to medium-low, and simmer for 45 minutes, uncovered.

5 Stir in the oregano, corn, black beans, chicken, and bacon. Season to taste with salt and pepper. Increase the heat to medium, and cook until heated through. Enjoy with the desired toppings!

shoyu ramen

Okay, I'm done with people being intimidated by ramen. The broth for tonkotsu-style ramen (not what you're making here) takes 12 to 24 hours to cook, which is exactly why most people don't even try. However, a good shoyu-style ramen like I have here can actually be done in as little as 1 hour. Not too bad, and you can really add any meat you like if you don't have chashu (page 167) on hand.

4 servings cooked
  straight ramen noodles

Tare (sauce):
½ cup (125ml) shoyu
3½ tbsp (50ml) mirin
1 (2–3-inch/5–7.5-cm)
  piece kombu

Soup base:
1 oz (25g) dried shiitake
  mushrooms
2½ cups (625ml) pork or
  chicken stock (see **basic
  stock out of anything,
  page 28**)
2 tbsp (30ml) neutral-
  tasting oil
2 tsp (10ml) toasted
  sesame oil
2-inch (5-cm) piece fresh
  ginger, peeled and
  minced
3 cloves garlic, minced
⅓ cup (75ml) sake
3 cups (750ml) **dashi
  (page 31)**
2 tsp (12g) kosher salt

Options for topping:
4–8 slices **chashu
  (page 167)**
4 **perfect soft-boiled
  eggs (page 90)**
2 green onions, sliced
Nori, cut into 1 x 2-inch
  (2.5 x 5-cm) pieces
Chili oil

1 Prepare the tare. In a small saucepan, combine all of the ingredients. Heat over medium heat until hot and steaming. Cover and let steep for 10 minutes, and discard the kombu. Transfer the tare to a separate container, and refrigerate to cool completely.

2 Prepare the soup base. Place the dried mushrooms in a medium bowl. In a medium saucepan, heat the pork or chicken stock over medium-high heat. As soon as it reaches a boil, pour the hot liquid over the mushrooms and cover the bowl with foil. Turn off the heat. Let steep and rehydrate for 10 to 15 minutes, or until the mushrooms are tender and cool enough to handle.

3 Remove the mushrooms, and squeeze them out over the water to catch the excess liquid. Place the mushrooms on a cutting board. Remove and discard the stems. Slice the mushroom tops into ¼-inch (0.5-cm) slices.

4 In a stockpot or Dutch oven, heat the neutral-tasting oil and sesame oil over medium heat. Once the oil begins to shimmer, add the ginger and garlic. Sauté just until fragrant and then stir in the sake. Increase the heat to medium-high, and boil until the liquid is about 90 percent evaporated. Then stir in the mushroom-pork (or chicken) stock, dashi, and salt. Reduce the heat to medium, and simmer for 10 minutes. Then strain the broth through a fine-mesh sieve, and discard the solids.

5 Assemble the ramen bowls. To each serving bowl, spoon in a couple tablespoons of the tare and then add the noodles on top. Ladle in broth to cover, and add the sliced rehydrated mushrooms and the toppings of choice. Taste and adjust tare seasoning levels to your liking. Enjoy!

PREP TIME:
**10 MINUTES + MAKING BUTTER, STOCK,
& GRILLED CHEESE (IF DESIRED)**

COOK TIME:
1 HOUR 20 MINUTES

SERVES:
4

tomato soup

Almost my entire life I hated tomato soup. But this tomato soup was a revelation to me. It's not weird and ketchup-tasting. It's herbaceous, fragrant, lightly tart, fresh, and just a touch on the creamy side. Plus, grilled cheese makes everything better.

2 lb (1kg) Roma tomatoes

3 tbsp (42g) **unsalted butter (page 33)**

4 cloves garlic, grated

2 shallots, finely chopped

1 sprig sage

2–3 cups (500–750ml) chicken stock (see **basic stock out of anything, page 28**)

½ cup (125ml) heavy whipping cream, plus more to serve

Kosher salt and freshly cracked black pepper, to taste

½ bunch of finely chopped chives

Grilled cheese (page 190; optional), cut into sticks, for dipping

1 Preheat the oven to 400°F (200°C). Halve the tomatoes and arrange in an even layer on a baking sheet. Roast cut-side down for 30 to 35 minutes, or until charred and soft.

2 In a large saucepan, melt the butter over medium heat. Add the garlic and shallots, and sauté until soft. Then add the roasted tomatoes, sage, and stock. Bring to a boil, reduce to a simmer, and cook for 30 to 40 minutes, or until the mixture is very soft.

3 Remove the sage. Stir in the heavy cream, and season to taste with salt and pepper. Transfer to a blender. Pulse until mostly smooth but some small chunks remain for texture, or to your desired consistency.

4 While still hot, transfer to serving bowls. Enjoy with a drizzle of heavy cream, fresh chives, freshly cracked black pepper, and grilled cheese sticks (if desired).

watermelon gazpacho

Every "food person" seems to have a watermelon gazpacho, so I'm just adding my name to the hat with this one. Once you sip on a nice chilled watermelon gazpacho while poolside on a scorching summer day, you'll finally understand why umbrella drinks are out of fashion. This is also a great palate cleanser before a nice meal.

1 English cucumber
1 serrano chili
4 cups cubed
   watermelon (about
   1.3 lb/600g total)
2 limes, divided
Kosher salt, to taste
½ cup (30g) mint leaves
½ cup (125ml) extra-
   virgin olive oil
¼ cup (5g) torn Thai
   basil leaves

1 Peel and seed half the cucumber. Cut the other half in a medium dice for garnish, and refrigerate until needed.

2 Over an open flame or with a blowtorch, char the chili until it's blackened on every side. Immediately place in a small container and cover with a lid to steam for 3 minutes. Then, using a paper towel, wipe off all the blackened bits and cut off the stem. If you prefer less heat, discard the seeds.

3 To a blender, add the chili, watermelon, seeded cucumber half, the zest and juice of 1 lime, and salt to taste. Blend on high speed until completely smooth. Taste and add more lime juice, if desired. Pour into a container, cover, and refrigerate for at least 1 hour.

4 While that's chilling, make the mint oil. Bring a small pot of water to a simmer over medium-high heat. Prepare an ice water bath. Submerge the mint leaves in the simmering water for 1 second and then immediately remove the leaves and submerge them in the ice water bath. Once the leaves are cold, place them on paper towels and gently squeeze them to remove as much moisture as possible.

5 To a blender, add the mint leaves and olive oil. Blend on high speed for about 30 seconds, or until the oil becomes a deep, dark green. Strain the mixture through a coffee filter set over a mesh strainer into a small container, and discard the pulp.

6 To serve, pour the chilled gazpacho into shallow serving bowls or glasses. Top with diced cucumber, zest of the remaining lime, Thai basil leaves, and a generous drizzle of the mint oil. Enjoy with a spoon, or drink from the glass.

SOUP

PREP TIME:
**5 MINUTES +
MAKING BROTH
(IF DESIRED)**

COOK TIME:
20 MINUTES

SERVES:
2

egg drop soup

When I was a kid, I used to order giant quart-sized containers of egg drop soup and absolutely drown it in an egregious amount of soy sauce until it was dyed a brownish root beer color (yeah, not nice). This delightfully salty, textured egg drop soup is to make amends for that troubled past.

2 cups (500ml) unsalted chicken stock (see **basic stock out of anything, page 28**)
1 whole star anise pod
1 tbsp (5g) toasted coriander seeds
1 tbsp (15ml) filtered water
2 tsp (5g) cornstarch
3 large eggs, whisked
2–3 tbsp (30–45ml) dark soy sauce (to taste)
1 tsp (5ml) toasted sesame oil
Thinly sliced green onion (optional), for garnish

1 In a medium saucepan, bring the chicken stock to a boil over medium-high heat and then reduce to a simmer over medium-low. Add the star anise and coriander seeds to a small piece of cheesecloth, and close with kitchen twine. Lower the cheesecloth into the boiling broth. Let simmer for 10 minutes and then remove the spices.

2 In a small bowl, whisk together the water and cornstarch. Stir the mixture into the broth. Simmer over medium-low heat for an additional 1 to 2 minutes, or until slightly thickened.

3 While stirring the broth slowly and constantly with chopsticks in one hand, slowly drizzle in the whisked eggs with the other hand. (I like to rest the tines of a fork over the rim of the egg bowl and pour the eggs through the tines to help slow the flow.)

4 Turn off the heat and let the soup sit undisturbed until the eggs are cooked through, about 2 minutes. Stir in the soy sauce and sesame oil. Garnish with green onion (if using), and enjoy!

dessert

Remember, it's spelled with the double "s" because it's so good you gotta go back for seconds. A terrible joke that's also true.

PREP TIME:
25 MINUTES + MAKING BUTTER (IF DESIRED)

COOK TIME:
35 MINUTES

YIELD:
1 DOUBLE-LAYER (9-INCH/ 23-CM) CAKE (SERVES 12–15)

the simplest chocolate cake

I used to loathe the idea of making a cake. It was just never something I was that interested in, and the pastry chefs I worked with always made it seem unnecessarily difficult. This recipe exists to show you otherwise.

2 cups (300g) unbleached all-purpose flour

¾ cup (80g) cocoa powder

2 tsp (10g) baking powder

¾ tsp (3g) baking soda

1½ tsp (7g) fine sea salt

1 cup (200g) granulated sugar

¾ cup (161g) firmly packed light brown sugar

2 large egg yolks

½ cup (125ml) neutral-tasting oil

1 tbsp (15ml) pure vanilla extract

2 large eggs

1¾ cups (425ml) whole milk

Dark chocolate (optional), for decorating

Frosting:

4 cups (500g) powdered sugar

½ cup (55g) cocoa powder

Generous pinch of fine sea salt

½ cup (112g) **unsalted butter (page 33),** softened

¼–½ cup (60–125ml) whole milk, to thin

1 Preheat the oven to 350°F (180°C). Grease the bottom of 2 (9-inch/ 23-cm) springform pans. Line the bottoms with parchment paper, and grease the parchment paper and walls of the pan.

2 Into a large bowl, sift the all-purpose flour, cocoa powder, baking powder, baking soda, and salt. Add the granulated sugar and brown sugar, and whisk until thoroughly combined.

3 In a medium bowl, whisk together the 2 egg yolks. While whisking continuously, slowly drizzle in the neutral-tasting oil just until it begins to thicken and emulsify and then whisk in the vanilla extract. Then continue to slowly drizzle in the remaining oil while whisking constantly.

4 Once all the oil has been added, add the 2 eggs and whisk to combine. Then pour the wet mixture into the dry ingredients and fold together until combined into a crumbly mixture.

5 In a small pot, heat the whole milk just until it begins to simmer, but do not let it boil. Once simmering, slowly pour the milk into the crumbly mixture while continuously whisking until everything is incorporated and smooth.

6 Divide the mixture evenly between the prepared cake pans. Bake for 30 to 35 minutes, or until a toothpick inserted into the center comes out clean. Let cool in the cake pans for 10 minutes.

7 Remove the sides of the pans, and carefully invert the cakes onto a wire rack. Remove the parchment paper from the bottoms. Let the cakes cool completely upside down. Prepare the frosting (see next page).

8 To frost the cakes, place 1 cake upside down on a cake stand or cutting board. Add about 1 cup frosting to the center, and spread it out evenly.

9 Place the second cake right-side up on top of the upside-down cake, and press down to make sure it sticks together. Spread the rest of the frosting on top and all over the sides to seal the edges.

10 Once the cake is completely frosted and covered, freshly grate dark chocolate on top of the cake (if using). Slice and enjoy!

11 To store, cover the cake with a large bowl or cake dome and let sit at room temperature for up to 2 days. Then refrigerate, covered, for 3 to 5 days.

Frosting:

In a medium bowl, whisk together the 4 cups (500g) powdered sugar, ½ cup (55g) cocoa powder, and a generous pinch of sea salt. In the bowl of a stand mixer or in a medium bowl, beat the ½ cup (112g) softened unsalted butter on medium speed until creamy. Add the powdered sugar mixture in batches until it is thoroughly combined with the butter. Thin out the frosting as desired using splashes of whole milk while the mixer is running until thick but spreadable.

PREP TIME:
50 MINUTES + 3 HOURS TO RISE +
MAKING BUTTER (IF DESIRED)

COOK TIME:
45 MINUTES

SERVES:
9

sticky buns

Does anything come to mind when you read the term *tangzhong?* Probably not sticky buns, let's be honest. To make a long story short, by cooking a small portion of flour and water together to make essentially a roux, you've made a tangzhong. It's a small but mighty addition to buns like this because you'll notice a significant bump in fluff and bloom to your breads when you pop in a bit of this magical starchy concoction.

Tangzhong:
1½ tbsp (14g) unbleached all-purpose flour
1½ tbsp (25ml) whole milk
1½ tbsp (25ml) filtered water

Dough:
½ cup (125ml) lukewarm milk, heated to about 98°F (37°C)
2½ tsp (9g) instant dry yeast
3 cups (450g) unbleached all-purpose flour
¾ tsp (2g) fine sea salt
3 tbsp (38g) granulated sugar
2 large eggs, room temperature
2½ tbsp (40ml) warm filtered water (if needed)
3½ tbsp (49g) **unsalted butter (page 33),** softened

Glaze:
½ cup (112g) **unsalted butter (page 33)**
½ cup (108g) firmly packed dark brown sugar
3 tbsp (64g) honey
1¼ cups (140g) toasted crushed pecans

Filling:
5 tbsp (70g) **unsalted butter (page 33),** gently melted
½ cup (108g) firmly packed dark brown sugar
2½ tsp (5g) ground cinnamon
Pinch of ground allspice
Pinch of freshly grated nutmeg

1 Make the tangzhong. In a medium saucepan, whisk together the flour, milk, and water until completely dissolved. Heat over medium heat, stirring continuously, until the mixture thickens into a thick paste. Transfer to a small bowl, and set aside to cool.

2 Start the dough. In a small bowl, add the milk. Stir in the yeast, cover with plastic wrap, and let sit for 10 minutes. The mixture should get lightly foamy, and the yeast should dissolve.

3 In the bowl of a stand mixer, whisk together the flour, salt, and sugar. Fit the mixer with the dough hook, and begin mixing the dry ingredients on medium-low speed. While the motor is running, 1 at a time, add the yeast mixture, the thickened and fully cooled tangzhong, and the eggs (1 egg at a time). Continue mixing on medium-low speed for 3 to 5 minutes, or until the dough is smooth and elastic. If dry, incorporate the warm water 1 teaspoon (5ml) at a time, adding up to 2½ tablespoons (40ml) total.

4 Increase the speed to medium, and mix in the butter 1 tablespoon (14g) at a time, allowing each addition to fully incorporate before adding the next. Once all of the butter is added, mix for an additional 5 minutes.

5 Remove the dough from the bowl, and gently shape it into a loose ball.

6 Lightly grease a medium bowl with cooking spray, and add the dough. Cover with greased plastic wrap. Allow to rise at room temperature for 1 to 2 hours, or until doubled in size.

7 Prepare the glaze. In a small pan, combine the butter, brown sugar, and honey. Heat over medium heat, stirring continuously, until thoroughly combined. Once combined, set aside to cool.

8 After the dough has doubled in size, punch down the dough to release the gas. Turn out onto a well-floured surface. Cover with a damp towel, and let rest for 10 minutes.

9 After 10 minutes, lightly flour the top of the dough and the surface beneath it. Using a rolling pin, roll the dough into a rectangle about 20 inches (51cm) long and ¼ inch (0.5cm) thick.

10 For the filling, brush the entire surface with the melted butter. In a small bowl, stir together the brown sugar, cinnamon, allspice, and freshly grated nutmeg until thoroughly combined. Sprinkle all of the cinnamon-sugar mixture evenly across the entire buttered surface, leaving a ¼-inch (0.5-cm) border.

11 From the long edge, roll the dough into a tight log. Lightly seal the top if possible. Trim about ½ inch (1.25cm) from the ends. Using a serrated knife, cut the dough at 2-inch (5-cm) intervals for a total of 9 equal rounds.

12 Grease a 9-inch (23-cm) square baking pan. Coat the bottom with the glaze. Sprinkle the toasted crushed pecans over the glaze. Arrange the rounds evenly spaced in rows of 3 on top of the pecans.

13 Cover the dish with a damp towel, and let proof at room temperature for 45 minutes to 1 hour, or until doubled in size. Once nearly done rising, preheat the oven to 350°F (180°C).

14 Bake for 30 to 35 minutes, or until the tops start to brown. Let sit at room temperature for 5 to 7 minutes. Gently loosen the buns, and invert them onto a plate or serving tray. Enjoy while still warm.

PREP TIME:
15 MINUTES + 30 MINUTES OR OVERNIGHT TO CHILL + MAKING BUTTER (IF DESIRED)

COOK TIME:
13–15 MINUTES

YIELD:
8

the ultimate chocolate chip cookie

Ah, the humble chocolate chip cookie. Not only is it the greatest type of cookie in the cookie world, but also one of my favorite sweets of all time. This one is my ideal version.

¾ cup (150g) granulated sugar
¾ cup (161g) firmly packed light brown sugar
1½ tsp (9g) fine sea salt
¾ cup (168g) **unsalted butter (page 33),** melted
1 large egg yolk
1 large egg
2 tsp (10ml) pure vanilla extract
1¼ cups plus 1 tbsp (197g) unbleached all-purpose flour
½ tsp (2g) baking soda
8 oz (225g) dark chocolate bar (about 70% cacao), roughly chopped

1 In a medium bowl, whisk together the granulated sugar, brown sugar, and salt. Whisk in the butter in a slow stream until completely combined and emulsified.

2 Whisk in the egg yolk, the whole egg, and the vanilla extract. Continue mixing until completely incorporated.

3 In a separate medium bowl, whisk together the flour and baking soda. Add the flour mixture to the sugar mixture. Gently mix together until just incorporated into a dough.

4 Fold in the chocolate. Cover the bowl with plastic wrap, and refrigerate for at least 30 minutes or ideally overnight.

5 Preheat the oven to 350°F (180°C). Line 2 baking sheets with parchment paper.

6 If the dough was in the refrigerator overnight, it may need to soften at room temperature for 5 to 10 minutes so it's relatively pliable but still very chilled. Using a medium-sized ice cream scoop (3–4 oz), spoon 4 large balls of dough onto 1 baking sheet at least 2½ inches (6.25cm) apart. Repeat on the other baking sheet.

7 Bake 1 sheet at a time for 13 to 15 minutes. When you have 10 minutes remaining in the bake time, pick up the sheet and gently drop it down onto the oven rack. (This will flatten the cookies slightly.) Repeat again when you have 7 minutes left, and once more when you have 3 minutes left. (This makes the cookies much chewier, fudgier, and richer.) Bake until the cookies are a light golden color on the outside but still just slightly underbaked on the inside.

8 Remove from the pan and cool completely on a wire rack. Enjoy! Store leftovers in an airtight container on the counter for up to 1 week.

PREP TIME:
**1 HOUR + ABOUT 2 HOURS FOR CHURNING +
OVERNIGHT FOR FREEZING**

COOK TIME:
30 MINUTES

YIELD:
5 CUPS

coffee ice cream

All the other ice creams do a really good job, and everyone has their favorite flavor. But have you ever noticed how intense people are about expressing their love of coffee ice cream? That's because it's the best. Making it yourself will not only caffeinate you, but also supply you with a custard-y, frozen, sweet treat version of a perfect cappuccino.

1¾ cups (150g) whole coffee beans

2 cups (500ml) whole milk

2 cups (500ml) heavy whipping cream, divided

1 cup (200g) granulated sugar

1¼ tsp (8g) kosher salt

6 large egg yolks

1   Freeze the base of the ice cream churner if needed according to the manufacturer's instructions. (Most ice cream makers require 24 hours for freezing, but if you don't want to wait, some ice cream makers come with a compressor so you don't have to freeze the base!)

2   Very lightly crush about half of the coffee beans into coarse pieces. In a medium pot, add the whole milk, 1 cup (250ml) heavy cream, the granulated sugar, and salt. Whisk in the whole and crushed coffee beans.

3   Place over low heat and slowly heat until steaming, but do not let it boil. Once steaming, cover with a lid and let it steep for 45 minutes over low to medium heat.

4   When it's almost done steeping, fill a large bowl with ice and water to create an ice bath. Place a smaller bowl inside the ice bath. To the small bowl, add the remaining 1 cup (250ml) heavy cream, and set aside.

5   After the coffee beans are done steeping, bring back up to steaming but not boiling. In a separate medium bowl, add the egg yolks. Ladle in a small amount of the steaming coffee cream, whisk together, and add another ladle of the coffee cream. Keep whisking to temper the eggs.

6   Whisk the yolk mixture into the pot of steaming coffee cream. Gently reheat it until steaming again, keeping it under 170°F (77°C). Maintain that heat while constantly whisking until it thickens enough to coat the back of a spoon, about 10 minutes.

7   Pour the custard through a fine-mesh sieve into the small bowl with the cream sitting in the ice bath, and stir. Cool the mixture until the custard is completely cold.

8   Add the ice cream base to the ice cream maker, and churn according to the manufacturer's instructions. Once the ice cream is fully churned, pour it into a few pints or an ice cream container. Freeze for a couple of hours or overnight. Enjoy!

PREP TIME:
45 MINUTES + OVERNIGHT TO FIRM + MAKING LADYFINGERS (IF DESIRED)

COOK TIME:
5 MINUTES

YIELD:
1 (9-INCH/23-CM) SQUARE PAN (ABOUT 9 SERVINGS)

tiramisu

My Italian friends are watching this recipe with great care and judgment.

¼ cup (50g) granulated sugar
2 cups (500ml) freshly brewed espresso or strong coffee, cold
3 tbsp (45ml) brandy or rum (optional)
Splash of pure maple syrup (optional)
Pinch of freshly grated nutmeg (optional)
24–30 **ladyfingers (page 82)**
Cocoa powder, for sifting
Dark chocolate, for grating

Zabaglione (tiramisu cream):
6–7 large egg yolks (depending on size of yolks)
¾ cup (150g) granulated sugar
2 cups (452g) mascarpone, room temperature
1 cup (250ml) heavy whipping cream

1 In a medium shallow dish, add the granulated sugar, espresso, the brandy or rum (if using), maple syrup (if using), and a pinch of nutmeg (if using). Whisk together until thoroughly combined. Set aside.

2 Make the zabaglione. Bring a medium pot filled with about 1 inch (2.5cm) of water to a light simmer over medium heat.

3 In a medium heatproof bowl that fits over the pot without touching the water, add the egg yolks and granulated sugar. Set the bowl over the steaming pot, and constantly whisk until most of the sugar is dissolved and the mixture is warm. Then, using a handheld mixer, beat on high speed while still heating over the double boiler until the mixture is 2½ times its original volume, much lighter in color, and holds soft peaks. Remove from the heat.

4 In a separate medium bowl, beat the mascarpone with a handheld mixer on medium speed until very smooth.

5 Add the mascarpone to the whipped egg yolk mixture, and gently fold until no lumps remain.

6 In the bowl that had the mascarpone, add the heavy whipping cream. Whip the cream until medium peaks are reached.

7 Add the egg-mascarpone mixture to the whipped cream, and gently fold together until thoroughly incorporated. Be very gentle to ensure it stays fluffy.

8 Dip the ladyfingers into the coffee mixture on both sides and instantly remove. Evenly line them up in a 9-inch (23-cm) square baking pan. Once the whole bottom is covered (they don't need to be placed too closely—gaps are okay), evenly pour over half of the zabaglione. Then add a final layer of dipped ladyfingers and the remaining zabaglione on top.

9 Cover the pan with plastic wrap, making sure it doesn't touch the mixture. Refrigerate overnight to firm.

10 Right before serving, generously dust the surface with cocoa powder. Slice the tiramisu, and grate the chocolate generously over top. Enjoy! Store leftovers tightly covered in the refrigerator for up to 3 days.

PREP TIME:
**25 MINUTES +
MAKING BUTTER
(IF DESIRED)**

COOK TIME:
10–12 MINUTES

YIELD:
2 DOZEN

russian tea cakes

Please understand there are a multitude of names for these and another slightly different version called Mexican wedding cookies. Yes, I know, very culturally confusing. And no, they're not actually cakes. They're more like little crumbly shortbread cookies, and they're damn delicious. I haven't seen a single holiday where my cousins and aunts didn't bring a mountain of these things and leave with an empty plate.

1 cup (224g) **unsalted butter (page 33)**, softened
½ cup (50g) sifted powdered sugar, plus more for coating
1 tsp (5ml) pure vanilla extract
2¼ cups (338g) unbleached all-purpose flour
2 tsp (12g) fine sea salt
¾ cup (97g) finely chopped raw hazelnuts

1 Preheat the oven to 400°F (200°C). Line a baking sheet with parchment paper. In a large bowl, using a handheld mixer, beat together the butter, powdered sugar, and vanilla on medium speed until light and creamy, 1 to 2 minutes.

2 In a medium bowl, whisk together the all-purpose flour and sea salt. Using a wooden spoon, stir the flour mixture into the butter mixture until it is a homogeneous dough.

3 Fold in the hazelnuts. Roll the dough into 1-inch (2.5-cm) balls and place on the baking sheet about 1 inch (2.5cm) apart. Bake the cookies for 10 to 12 minutes, or until just set. While they're baking, fill a small bowl with powdered sugar to coat the cookies.

4 Once the cookies are cool enough to handle but still very warm, roll each of them in the powdered sugar. Place the coated cookies on a wire rack to cool completely. Sprinkle more powdered sugar over top, if desired. Enjoy! Store leftovers in an airtight container on the counter for up to 4 days.

PREP TIME:
**30 MINUTES + MAKING
BUTTER (IF DESIRED)**

COOK TIME:
15–17 MINUTES

YIELD:
8

strawberry shortcake

I haven't spent a ton of time making strawberry shortcake, and I've always thought it to be a rather boring dessert. I only knew the commercial version, which is primarily a cake or crumbly bread. That is, until I discovered the biscuit version, which isn't just easy to make, but it's also the only version that should exist.

1lb (450g) strawberries, hulled and sliced

4 tbsp (50g) granulated sugar, divided

1 tbsp (13g) muscovado or dark brown sugar

Small pinch of sea salt

1 cup (250ml) heavy whipping cream

Biscuits:

3 cups (450g) unbleached all-purpose flour, plus more for dusting

¼ cup (50g) granulated sugar

2 tbsp (21g) baking powder

1 tsp (6g) fine sea salt

¾ cup (168g) **unsalted butter (page 33),** cold, cubed

1 cup (250ml) buttermilk, cold, plus more for brushing

1 large egg yolk

Zest of 1 lemon

Demerara sugar, for sprinkling

1 In a large bowl, combine the strawberries, 3 tablespoons (38g) granulated sugar, the muscovado sugar, and a pinch of salt. Toss together until evenly combined. Refrigerate until ready to use.

2 Prepare the biscuits. In a medium bowl, whisk together the all-purpose flour, granulated sugar, baking powder, and salt until thoroughly combined. Add the flour mixture to a food processor, along with the cold cubed butter. Pulse a few times until pea-sized crumbs of butter are formed.

3 Pour the mixture back into the original bowl, and add the buttermilk, egg yolk, and lemon zest. With a spoon, mix together until it forms a dough.

4 Turn the dough onto an unfloured surface, and lightly knead just until it comes together. Don't overwork the dough; it's okay if it's a little shaggy.

5 Roll the dough out into a roughly 10-inch- (25-cm-) long rectangle. Fold like a letter (into thirds over itself), roll it out lengthwise, and fold like a letter once more. Wrap in plastic wrap and refrigerate for 10 minutes. While it's resting, preheat the oven to 425°F (220°C), and line 2 baking sheets with parchment paper or silicone baking mats.

6 Dust a surface with flour, and roll out the dough until it's about ½ inch (1.25cm) thick. Using a 3½-inch (9-cm) biscuit cutter, cut out as many biscuits as possible, about 8, rerolling the scraps as able.

7 Arrange the biscuits on the baking sheets. Brush the tops with buttermilk, and sprinkle with demerara sugar. Bake for 15 to 17 minutes, or until beautifully golden brown. Remove the biscuits from the oven, and let cool completely before using.

8 When ready to assemble, prepare the whipped cream topping. In a medium bowl, whip the heavy cream and remaining 1 tablespoon (12g) granulated sugar with a whisk until moderately stiff peaks form.

9 To assemble each shortcake, split a biscuit in half. On the bottom half, top with whipped cream and add a spoonful of strawberries with some of their juice on top. Top with the other half of the biscuit. If desired, spoon on more whipped cream and another spoonful of strawberries and their juice. Enjoy!

DESSERT

PREP TIME:
**15 MINUTES + MAKING BUTTER
& PEANUT BUTTER (IF DESIRED)**

COOK TIME:
12–14 MINUTES

YIELD:
1 DOZEN

peanut butter cookies

Wait, where are the fork marks? (I know you just thought that. I'm in your head.) These aren't the crumbly, ridged peanut butter cookies you already know. These are the soft and chewy kind—the kind that make you cry a little peanut buttery tear from the textured wonderland you experience in each bite.

2¼ cups (338g) unbleached all-purpose flour

1½ tsp (6g) baking soda

1½ tsp (9g) fine sea salt

1 cup (215g) firmly packed light brown sugar

½ cup (100g) granulated sugar

1 cup (224g) **unsalted butter (page 33),** gently melted

1 cup (256g) creamy peanut butter (see **nut butters, page 26**)

2 large eggs

2 tsp (10ml) pure vanilla extract

Turbinado sugar, to coat

1   Preheat the oven to 350°F (180°C), and line 2 baking sheets with parchment paper. In a medium bowl, whisk together the all-purpose flour, baking soda, and salt until incorporated.

2   In a separate medium bowl, whisk together the brown sugar and granulated sugar. While constantly whisking, slowly add the melted butter in a stream, followed by the peanut butter, eggs, and vanilla.

3   Add the flour mixture to the sugar mixture, and whisk until thoroughly combined.

4   Add the turbinado sugar to a bowl for coating. Roll the dough into 12 evenly sized balls (about 3.5 oz/100g each), and roll in the sugar until generously coated. Arrange the balls on the baking sheets at least 2 inches (5cm) apart. Press each ball gently with your palm or the bottom of a flat cup to slightly flatten.

5   Bake for 12 to 14 minutes, or until lightly golden. Remove from the pan and cool completely on a wire rack. Enjoy! Store leftovers in an airtight container on the counter for up to 3 days.

index

acknowledgments

A thank you I try to repay every day—to my supporters. I'm not even really sure what to call you guys. Fans? Readers? Viewers? Audience members? You, the person reading this right now...there isn't a day that goes by I'm not hustling to provide more value for you. Without your support, I'm not sure any of my dreams could have been possible. From the bottom of my heart, thank you so much. There is MUCH more to come, and I couldn't be more thankful to have you all on my side. Whoever you are, please know how important you are to me.

Thank you to my lady Katherine for taste-testing and letting me bother you with the progress of my book while you were working through law school like a mad woman! I'm unbelievably grateful for your excitement and support.

Thank you to everyone in my family who has always been unbelievably supportive and excited for everything I do with food. You guys know who you are. It's the collective power and excitement my family provides around food that has shaped my direction.

Thank you to all of my restaurant industry friends who came to help make this book a reality by supporting me through the photo shoot. Damon Cook, Yuma Herrera, Cameron Gaab, and Daniel Castro, you guys are rock stars, and I look forward to seeing you all grow.

A massive thank you to my growing small-but-mighty team: Vicram Chatterjee and Thomas Werner. You guys are not only part of the beginning of something amazing, but you've added an unbelievable amount of value in a way I never could have expected. Vicram, I really am just so proud and grateful for the way you've taken hold of your place here. In everything you do, you go above and beyond, and more importantly, you are just an amazing human and a constant ray of positivity. You've become one of my right-hand men, and I'm excited for what's to come. TJ, I am so grateful for how quickly and perfectly you've fit into the mix of things here. We're ecstatic to have you as our partner in crime as we grow through all of this. I'm happy to call you both teammates, but I'm even happier to call you good friends.

Thank you to all the chefs who've been patient with me and given up absolutely priceless advice and knowledge throughout my experience in restaurants. I'm still pushing to learn more, apply more, and help evolve the food industry, and I will never stop.

Thank you to my managers, Joshua Cohen and Brian Sokolik, for not only sticking by me, but for fighting for me, not just as managers, but as friends and people who believe in me. Love you guys.

Thank you to Ian and everyone at Regalis for providing all the specialty items for this book. I love you guys! If anyone is interested in any type of hard-to-find specialty ingredient, check out Regalis Foods at regalisfoods.com.

And finally to my parents. When I told them I wasn't going to college several years ago, they didn't stop me. They believed in me, but internally I knew it stung a little for them, especially for my mom, who had always dreamed of having her son go to a prestigious university because many of her family never had the opportunity. That unwavering support is a perfect example of how much of a priority they have made my happiness and my freedom to discover my own path. They bought me my first set of knives the moment I started cooking. My mom taught me how to cook anything I wanted to learn. She also taught me how to teach myself cooking techniques. They acquired (reasonably) anything I needed to get better at the craft of cooking. My dad helped me understand how my passion could be financially viable so I wasn't living with a starving artist mentality. They even bought me a whole pig when I was 16 because I wanted to learn proper whole animal butchery. (To say the least, my mom was visibly concerned when she walked into the living room to see that in action...serial killer vibes?) I feel a strong sense of urgency to find ways to repay them, and although I haven't figured out that fully, I hope this thank you is a good start. This book is 110% dedicated to you both. This is just the beginning, and I'm not stopping, not even when I get to where I want to go. I've come a long way, and none of it would be a reality without the unbelievable amount of love, support, and patience from both of you. I love you more than anything, even cooking.

DK would like to thank the following individuals at Ralph Smith Studios for their involvement in the photo shoot:

Ralph Smith, photographer
Dee Statiras, prop stylist, project coordinator
Kathleen Pyle, prop stylist
McKenzie Emmott, food stylist
Steve Lanman, post-production retoucher

about
the author

Joshua Weissman isn't your average culinary genius. He's chef-y, he's eccentric, and he's a lot over-the-top in everything he does—from curating energetic and engaging food entertainment, to constantly developing his massive repertoire of original recipes, to cooking everything (seriously, everything) from scratch.

He has an abounding love of food and proper technique. After nearly a decade of cooking professionally, his passion has been fueled by working with some of the greatest fine dining restaurants in the south-central region of the United States. He notably cooked at the James Beard Award–winning restaurant Uchiko, where he spent time focusing on the finest details of cuisine, training other cooks and chefs, and diving deep into the territory of precise Japanese cookery and fermentation.

Joshua can be seen chopping it up for millions of fans on his popular YouTube channel, Facebook, TikTok, and Instagram. He currently resides in Texas and plans to push the world of food further than it has ever gone before.